Providing Comfort

by

Lance A. Walker

Bloomington, IN   Milton Keynes, UK

AuthorHouse™
1663 Liberty Drive, Suite 200
Bloomington, IN 47403
www.authorhouse.com
Phone: 1-800-839-8640

AuthorHouse™ UK Ltd.
500 Avebury Boulevard
Central Milton Keynes, MK9 2BE
www.authorhouse.co.uk
Phone: 08001974150

This book is a work of fiction. People, places, events, and situations are the product of the author's imagination. Any resemblance to actual persons, living or dead, or historical events, is purely coincidental.

First published by AuthorHouse 11/16/2006

ISBN: 978-1-4259-7210-3 (sc)

Printed in the United States of America
Bloomington, Indiana

This book is printed on acid-free paper.

Library of Congress Control Number: 2006909348

Edited by Mary Daniels

A PILOT'S FAITH

We all know *the risks of our lives and professions. We must take everything we have learned, calculate our chances, say our prayers, and do our duty.*

We know at any second we could meet our fate in a fireball. Still, we do our heart's desire, stopping only for a second to remember life isn't forever anyway.

And if by some twist of fate we find ourselves in a no-win situation, then we will cling to our beliefs and carry our faith beyond impact...

L.A. Walker

DEDICATION

To God, that has, and still is, providing comfort.

To my wife and children that care for me at my worse.
To my parents that sent a boy to the Army, and welcomed home a veteran.

To all those, still out there so we can be here.

INTRODUCTION

The Gulf War was a war that ended too fast for some and too late for others, but for many that war has not yet ended.

In the spring of 1991 there were over 60,000 Kurdish refugees in the mountains of Northern Iraq, having fled for their lives. Yet the United States decided to leave Saddam in power. He had imposed a harsh sentence of extermination on any group opposing his brutal reign. Saddam killed thousands of Kurds with nerve gas, artillery, firing squads, and starvation. That spring the United States stepped in and rescued what was left of the Kurdish people. Stuck in the middle of an age-old dispute, the U.S. had to stay friends with the Turks—who are also enemies of the Kurds—while rescuing and arming the Kurds to oppose the Iraqi government. It was the hope of the U.S. government that the Kurdish people would be able to overthrow Saddam.

The United States decided to send in two separate operations under the name of "Operation Provide Comfort". The first, a massive humanitarian relief to rescue the Kurds; the second, a special operations contingent to train the Kurdish people and wage a black operations war against what was left of Saddam's brutal dictatorship. That's where the American attack pilots and special operation soldiers came in.

To find that special few, the army searched the small towns and cities with specially designed ads on T.V, in books, and at post offices. These ads were designed to attract young men and women with a severe love of flying and adventure. Once attracted, they would sell their futures to the army for a chance to be one of the few to fly a vague machine.

For every one that made it, there were a thousand that didn't. And for those who were accepted to flight school, one out of six got his wings.

The army recruited, tested, and screened, trying to find that certain personality profile that could make a soldier, officer, and aviator.

I was one of those…

As I deployed and served in Iraq, every event became a valuable lesson. Through my life's journey, I chose the path that led me here, writing to you. As your eyes follow these words across the page, may you find something here beyond war and adventure. Maybe you will also see the force that guided and protected me along the razor's edge of high-adventure flying and dangerous combat missions. That force might have been a small voice inside, or a seeming twist of fate, or luck, or the mighty hand of God gently providing comfort. You decide.

These are my notes.........

Some are born to move the world
To live their dreams,
But most just dream about
The things they would like to be.

Move the world.
Live your dreams.

Let us pray for those brave souls
Who never stop and count the risks
Of stepping out of the mold of norm
To defy the fear of failure.

Proving to us all
That our dreams are waiting for us
Just beyond our fears...

L.A. Walker

CHAPTER ONE
HIGH STANDARDS

Slow, clean drops of rain from an overcast sky was a sharp contrast to my life in the war. The life there was more unreal than real. Dry, powdery dust left me with an unquenchable thirst and cotton mouth, longing for just a touch of water on my lips. Here it rained crystal clear drops of sweet water. There, it was so dry that a drop of blood turned to a brown stain in seconds, life draining into the sand, easily kicked to dust.

Here I reveled in the smell of rain and cut grass. There, no grass, just the smell of stale dust, coupled with the acrid smell of burning trash, plastic, and sometimes flesh. And overall, the sweet aroma of gun solvent.

Gun solvent and cold steel. I remembered the handle of a knife fitting snug and tight in my grip, providing a cold comfort. Its blade, like my mind, was honed to a razor-sharp edge. I remembered too my nine mm pistol that fit in my hand as if its handgrip was custom carved. The Beretta with its easy hold was a best friend and companion, always cleaned, checked and rechecked, then slid away and holstered under my right arm. It waited there patiently for that time when life is hurried and time is measured in rationed seconds. When your heart beats heavily and reality becomes blurred. When adrenaline hits the bloodstream and your actions become subconscious When your eyes watched your hands perform, preprogrammed years ago at a training facility thousands of miles away where time was plentiful. Sight alignment, trigger squeeze, fast but sure. Target up, squeeze, explosion, target down. Target, man, enemy, all the same. Ears ringing, trigger squeeze, pop, sights rise with every pop, falling across another only to pop again. My hands performed again and again as the steel heated up, releasing the smell of gun powder and solvent.

The private audience behind my eyes graded each shot. Head shot, eye shot, body crumpled in a pile on the ground. Silhouettes up, sights align, slack already out of the trigger, explosion, pile, brown sand. My hands directed the cold steel, dismissing life, making choices. Whether my choice or no choice, my path had led me here where I began. Temporary tracks across the sand, permanent impressions in my mind, hidden behind the face that stares out of this mirror on the bathroom wall.

Was I ready for my future as a civilian? Perfection comes in many different forms. Buttons all buttoned and aligned with zipper and belt buckle. Trousers pressed, the crease sharp and defined, almost sharp enough to cut. The suit is freshly cleaned, no lint, dark, distinguished. My tie is a deep burgundy, tied tight with a Windsor knot, and hanging precisely two fingers above the belt. Army regulation, of course. Perfection. My face is smoothly shaved with no nicks. Nose hairs, none; ear hairs, none. I am clean cut. But was the mirror telling the truth? Was I ready for my first "out of the Army" job interview?

"Mr. Walker, you can fill out this application and return it to the front desk? We will call you in a little while to interview with Captain Neeley. We will also keep your application on file for ninety days. But just to let you know, most of our officers are selected from the ranks. I know you said you were in the army and all, but everybody has been in something or other, and besides we train better here in the department. Yes, I've heard of Special Operations, and to tell you the truth, that doesn't make a hill of beans difference here. This is a totally different ball game. Like I said before, we hire from our jail staff or reserves here. You can leave an application, but remember we have several dozen people in front of you and the deputy pilot position is very competitive."

Her voice drifted off somewhere into the distance as I watched the traffic at the Sheriff's Office. I picked out a subject, an older deputy, overweight, sloppy. His uniform would fail the most basic inspection, the weapon on the pistol belt was dusty, probably hadn't been fired in months. His haircut was rough; his shoes needed a shine. Probably never even owned a pair of running shoes. My overall evaluation of this individual: unsatisfactory. But who was I to judge? Only the events will judge him on that special day when he would find himself up against someone who was willing to give it all, and to take it all, maybe his life or just his pride. Who was I to judge?

My next subject was a female in uniform behind the desk, her hair neat and her uniform clean. But her speech was clipped and she was condescending to those she addressed. She had something to prove.

But who was I to judge? Hopefully she would never have the opportunity to prove what she could do. Upper body strength, weak, shooting judgment, hesitant. Over confident to the point of self-defeating. Probably would miss that one individual who would show weakness just to appease her, then in the next second, break her neck with quick-trained hands. He would remember those orders she barked at him, while he laughed inside at her foolish arrogance.

Who was I to judge? Here in this little place maybe they would never be judged.

The judge was final and showed no mercy. He came when one least expected him; he knew all your weaknesses, your thoughts and fears, and he rendered a decision that simply showed, trained or untrained, death or life with a lasting memory of what to train for next. This unit didn't need a guy like me. Recruited from within. Six years of my life spent training. Three million dollars of the people's money spent on detail-oriented training. Sharpening perfection. Not needed here. What counted in civilian life? My sanity, slipping. Maybe it never happened. All the hours, sweat, tears and blood. Brown stains left in the sand in some lost place on a map. Was I there? All the dreams, the sweats, the crazy thoughts, restless feelings in crowds. Nights of walking the floor, walking the yard, staring out the window, ready. For what? Why? Self-training to the point of obsession. Shooting and shooting until all rounds fit under a dime. Running till the mile passed in under six minute. Sweat, tears. Why was I not qualified? Would anyone give an Apache pilot a chance? I was either over-qualified to sweep the floors or under-qualified to be a deputy. Old words from one of my instructors flashed across my mind,

"Son, God and soldier are adored in time of fright, but easily forgotten in time of delight."

Delight. These people were sitting here in good ole USA in delight. They didn't have a clue to the rest of the world. Of pilots on a mission, of a Delta operator making head shots, of SEALs saving some civilian that has been kidnapped. Always out there at the edge of my mind, carved in my memory with a sharp red hot knife, cut deep, leaving a ugly scar…

Out there…

CHAPTER TWO
IN THE BEGINNING

KUWAIT 1990

The early dawn sky had a light pink glow, becoming red as the minutes ticked by on the alarm clock set to go off at six a.m.

At six he would hit the snooze. At fifteen minutes past six he would get up; by six thirty, he would be dressed.

He would kiss his sleeping wife good-bye, look in on his two children, and be in the oil fields by seven. This had been his everyday routine. But not today.

Today, a buzzing sound woke him. As he reached to hit the alarm, he noticed it was only four a.m. and the alarm still hadn't sounded. A bright light shone into the bedroom from outside. Just as the man stood to put on his clothes, the door was blasted off its hinges. Before the man could identify who or what was invading his home, he felt a burning in his chest. The floor hit him in the back. It was hard to breath. Air filled his lungs, but not through his mouth. He felt a warm sensation running under his back. Somewhere in the fading area of his senses he thought he heard a woman scream. It sounded like his wife. Then a child screamed.

"Oh, God!" he called.

His vision was momentarily bright and clear, but seemed to dim every other second. There was another sound, a foreign sound.

"No it can't be!" he thought.

But it was. Iraqi voices. He concentrated, but his hearing was fading along with his sight. A bone-chilling scream came from somewhere in the room then faded to an echo in his mind. He took a breath but could not exhale. His vision blurred, cleared, and blurred again. Then all was dark.

April 1991
Insurlik Air base, Turkey

Sun baked the asphalt runway, giving view to a mirage of shimmering heat waves across the line of helicopters. The little breeze that brushed my face felt as if it was born in an oven. It was hot and sweltering. Any metal object in this heat would burn to the touch, including the seatbelts. My gloves were best served on my hands when negotiating a seatbelt left uncovered in this heat. I fumbled with my five-point harness at the same time Mitch does.

The order had come, Mitch is sure of it. As his mind pondered the idea of war, his hands methodically traced down the startup checklist to the Apache helicopter. With the flip of the APU switch the auxiliary power unit blasted to life with a low roar.

Seconds later, cold air blew from the air-conditioning vents and slowly dried the sweaty glaze that covered our faces. I looked up into the rear cockpit mirror to see if Mitch was finished with his checks. When he finished, he would look into the mirror to see if I was finished with the front seat duties.

Today he was slower than normal. Mitch tuned the radios to tower frequency with his left hand as he adjusted the picture of his wife and three children with his right hand. Our group was designated to be part of a special operations unit. The Army had assembled our unit from scratch. Half of our pilots were straight from flight school, the other half were seasoned veterans.

Mitch Reaves, with his thinning salt and pepper hair now hidden under his flight helmet, was wondering how this war will turn out. The last war Mitch flew in was Vietnam.

"It would be nice to have sit this one out," Mitch silently thought as he glanced down at the picture of the wife and kids he never saw. Flipping the starter switch to start, Mitch gently placed his lovely family in their neat little mental compartment in the back of his mind. Of course he could think of them anytime he felt lonely, but at this moment it was time to put an aircraft into the air, and there was never enough room for thinking of anything but flying.

Mitch shut his mental compartment and gently pushed the starter switch to the detent

"And the sleeping dragon awakes," came a voice over the intercom.

"Are you ready to beat the air into submission young aviator?" Chief Warrant Officer Mitch Reaves asks as he pulled his dark visor over his face. We fellow aviators called him Super Man.

I was seated in front: Chief Warrant Officer Lance Walker. My nickname was none other than "SkyWalker", but I was called "Luke" for short.

Today was the last day before we reach Iraq. We had been flying from Illeshiem, Germany. Our unit was assembled in Fort Hood Texas, deployed to Germany, and had traveled over 3,000 miles and five countries. Tomorrow we entered the combat zone of Northern Iraq, that place they called no-man's land. When we arrived we would not officially be in war. Desert Storm had ended several months ago. Our mission would be to conduct operations in Northern Iraq intended to protect the Kurdish refugees from Iraqi aggression. But little did I know this would be more than that. This mission would be a combat mission, and something more. Something the U.S. government didn't tell the world. The control tower operator's voice entered my ear, telling me we were cleared for take-off. With the slight pull of my left hand on the collective, the rumble of the rotor blades dissipated with the scattered dust as we lifted off into the royal blue sky over Turkey. Our flight would last about four hours before we landed in Zakho, Iraq.

As Mitch finished his backseat level-off checks, I quickly checked my navigation system with the ten-year-old map to be sure we were headed in the right direction.

The view of Eastern Turkey was stunning from five thousand feet. As we flew, I tried to imagine all the history that was born here. Somewhere north lay the remains of Noah's ark. South of here was the Mediterranean and Syria. And here we were in the middle, flying above the cradle of mankind, a symbol of the past and present on the edge of the future. Just out my right window there were four hellfire missiles hanging next to thirty-six hydra 70 folding-fin rockets. On my left were four more hellfire missiles, but with a large fuel tank in the place of the rocket pod. Under my feet were twelve hundred rounds of

30-mm cannon ammunition for the gun on the front of this bird. This gun was slaved to my head movements, so I could simply look at a target, squeeze the trigger, and send six hundred and fifty rounds per minute of 30-mm bullets to destroy it. All this firepower. And to think I was flying it into battle for the most powerful nation on earth.

I checked the rear cockpit mirror to see Mitch looking out his side window. He must have been enjoying the same thing I was. Tomorrow we could both be gone, but today we were flying the meanest machine on the planet and enjoying the most beautiful scenery on earth. I wished I could show my children and family all this beauty. For this was indeed a beauty only seen from this spot.

Just as this thought hit me, I pull out my Cannon Snappy from my left leg pocket and snapped a picture. The sun melted into the mountains behind us, casting a bright orange tint on the sky above as the Doppler navigation systems told me we were now two hours into our flight, disappearing into the falling curtain of night.

"Hey you awake up there?"

"Not before you read me a night time story."

"Just checking!"

"I'm just enjoying all this beauty. I wouldn't miss all this for the world. Besides, there aren't many scenes like this where I come from."

"Where do you come from?" Mitch asked.

"Branford Florida," I answered, fully expecting him to not have a clue about the little town in North Florida on the banks of the Suwannee River.

"It must be small," he said, guessing from my country accent.

"Real small," I answered with my best Southern draw.

"How in the world did a country plowboy make it to fly Apache helicopters? You must have had some flying experience or a pilot's license," he asked with a genuine interest.

Mitch had spent several years in the Army as a crew chief. He then requested the Warrant Officer Program and was accepted after his third application.

"Some flying, a lot of persistence and not understanding the word no," I replied.

I could feel him silently wondering if I was just shooting him a line. As he wondered, I drifted back to that boy I was. The boy that was bitten by the flying bug.

I was on our family farm in Branford, Florida. The large blue Ford tractor belched black smoke into the clean Florida air as the twelve-year-old boy piloted it down each row of cut hay. The hay bailer scratched and clang as it sucked the hay in, winding it into a nice neat bail. Sweat dripped off my nose as the southern sun beat against my back.

Across the field several white birds glided in to catch any grasshoppers they could find behind the hay bailer. I watched the birds, noting how they seemed to easily balance themselves on the air. They floated, drifted, and glided with ease. I thought how much I would love to be like them, to master the air, to go wherever and whenever I pleased with no earthly bonds, to fly straight up, or stop and land on a bail of hay. I checked my watch. It was almost time for them to make their daily run. There they were, right on time. I stopped the tractor and stood in amazement. The sleek fighter jets passed like a blur no more than fifty feet over the top of the tractor. With the velocity of a rocket, they ripped the air and shook the ground, completely drowning out the sound of the tractor and hay bailer. They displaced the air around me, my breath seemed to be taken away and my heart skipped several beats from the shock wave.

"What a rush!" I said aloud. I waved my arms frantically, hoping to get some response from my mentors.

The jets screamed away leaving a black trail. The smell of burnt jet fuel settles over the field. Chills ran down the my back.

"Yes!" I screamed. "Yes! That's me!"

Across the field my father heard the screams. Thinking something was wrong, he jumped into his pickup truck and raced to the spot where I stood on the tractor.

"What in the hell is wrong?" my father asked.

"Did you see those jets? They were A-7 Corsairs, U.S. Navy, dad!"

"I don't give a damn if they are bombing us, I want your butt to stay on that tractor!" my father yelled, his face red and with an intense fire in his eyes. As the evening settled the dust of the hay field, I drove the tractor from the back forty to the barn. My mind floated into the bright orange sunset displayed across the darkening Florida sky. I wondered how I could ever get there. Get to where the sun was setting. Get to those places only shown on television and in movies. Get to here flying into combat.

My Doppler began blinking; we were thirty minutes from Iraq.

"Roger, let's make a call!" I said, snapping out of my daydream.

Mitch began calling the AWAC's radar plane controlling the skies over Iraq.

"NorthStar, This is Bushwacker 29, west of Dodge City. Requesting passage and vectors to Dodge."

"Bushwacker, this is Northstar, radar contact, you're cleared to Dodge. Be advised severe weather approaching from the north. Your final vector is 095. Have a good night."

AWAC was basically telling us to fly a heading of 095 and look for Zakho, Iraq.

"I'm descending. Go ahead and put on your night vision system. It looks like we are going to need it," I said, as I lowered the aircraft from five thousand to one thousand feet.

The sky was black, real black. The stars that were out earlier were now gone. The ground lights were also starting to fade ahead of us. I knew what this was. So did Mitch. A fast moving storm was about to cross the path we had to take. There was no place to land. Mountains stand as a wall to the north. Syria stretches to the South. I could only wonder what was below. We had to fly a 095 heading or we would crash or be shot down.

"Do you see what I see?" I asked, already knowing Mitch's answer.

"Yes, a wall of pitch-black something!" Mitch said with a reluctant calmness.

Just as Mitch spoke, it hit us. The aircraft shook and buffeted. Mud and rain splattered on the windshield. The night vision system was our only visual contact with the ground.

"This is a not-good mess!" Mitch mumbled through his clinched teeth.

"News flash! My night system is going out!" I said, as I flipped several switches trying to optimize the view.

We had trained for accidentally flying into bad weather, but never in a combat theater of operations.

There was no inadvertent IMC here. Our fuel was critical, only about thirty minutes left. Our only choice is to fly straight and level on 095 until our Doppler said we were close or we at least ran out of this storm.

We were the last of eighteen Apaches to arrive in Zakho. Our entire unit was down there on the ground, if only we could find them.

"My system is out!" Mitch yelled. This was not good news. This meant we were officially blind. I said a small prayer. For what seemed like forever, but probably only several minutes, we flew blind. Just as quick as my prayer had touched the edge of Heaven, some lights appeared on the horizon. "I've got lights, twelve o'clock." came Mitch's relieved voice over the intercom. "Thank you God!" I said out loud. Then I said another thank-you silently.

"I see the base, I got the controls." Mitch took the controls and banked the Apache into a tight right turn and lined up with the chemical stick lights arranged in a large Y pattern on the ground.

An eerie feeling fell over me as I began to take in the outline of the base. From what I could make out in the pitch dark, the landing area and so-called base had a large wall of dirt around it. On both sides of the wall was rolled razor wire. It looked like a makeshift prison. All the buildings were partially destroyed. Some had strange

Arabic writing on them, others were just simply painted white.

I pulled off my flight helmet and gloves, just as a crew chief opened my cockpit door.

"Sir, when you get your stuff, you will need to follow me exactly because this area isn't completely swept for land minds. Oh, by the way, welcome to Iraq!"

One hundred and fifty steps later we entered into one of the long block building with a tent top.

"It's about time! We done shot all the Iraqis!" There he was, Bugs Bunny. I didn't realize how much I missed him. Ed Hammock. "Bugs."

CHAPTER THREE
Making Friends

Bugs and I were best friends. We were roommates in Texas and classmates at flight school. He was about the ugliest person I had ever seen, but he was one of the best pilots in the Army.

Bugs had large protruding front teeth, giving him the nickname Bugs. I don't guess it takes looks to fly. Bugs and I loved each other like brothers and fought like brothers. Bugs and I met the first day of flight school. It was at Fort Rucker, Alabama, in 1988. That was three years ago, but it seems like yesterday.

It was our third day of Warrant Officer candidate training. A candidate named Virgil was doing pushups for the TAC officer and getting slower. I could tell he was tired. Anybody would be tired. His arms trembled from the pressure of his slightly over-weight frame.

The TAC Officer got down on his knees in the mud next to the rapidly wilting Warrant Officer candidate and said, "Why are you here? Don't do this for anyone else. You've got to want it, I mean really want it! You've got to want it more than you love yourself. You have to make your soul bleed for it."

Another TAC sprayed water and splashed more mud on Virgil.

"Your a slug!" The TAC whispered through his gritted teeth.

"I can make it all go away in a matter of seconds, all you have to do is quit. You can be home for the weekend. Out of this torturous hell and home drinking tea."

I listened as I stood at rigid attention feeling tired and somewhat homesick. I knew I would never quit. It would be better to go back to Branford in a box than a quitter. The TAC officer almost had Virgil at the quitting point. The TAC had his job to do. Virgil, with no sleep in the last two days was about to give up and throw away years of hard work. He was completely broken down. His arms gave away as he fell on his face in the mud. The TAC zeroed in for Virgil's resignation. Virgil raised his muddy face with tears streaming, his teeth gritting in the mud. He was exhausted. I couldn't stand to see my classmate in such distress. Just the day before he had told me about his dream to be a pilot. He wanted to make his parents proud of him. He told me he was from New York and would return there after graduation for a couple of weeks and get married. Now here he was about to resign. I could see the fire in his eyes fading. And for a brief second, I could hear my dad in the back of my mind. "Don't be weak! It's all a mental game. Life is what you make it."

Virgil's watery eyes begged for help. At that second, my veins filled with fire and ice all at the same time. While standing at attention in a perfect line with all the other candidates, I moved just enough to catch the TAC officer's eye. I knew Virgil wouldn't last and I would. The TAC Officer froze. He turned and looked at me. Then he moved in my direction like a mountain lion going in for the kill. I braced. He was inches from my face. His breath had the stench of onions. Any other time, it would have made me tremble to have the TAC screaming at me. Now, I am tired, mad, and feeling that he might eat me, but not swallow me whole.

Through gritted teeth he interrogated me, "Did you move, Candidate Walker?"

"Sir, Candidate Walker, Yes Sir!" I sounded off while still looking straight forward, trying to ignore his breath.

He sneered at me, then grinned.

"I see. We have a bleeding heart here, a crusader. He cares more about this slob in the mud than he does his own hide."

The TAC paced in front of me. Then he told Virgil to get up and go sit down and rest. The TAC turned to me and screamed,

"DROP!"

Without even thinking, I was in the push-up position. After the first sixty-five push-ups, my arms were begging for a break. The TAC yelled and I counted out loud.

Just as I couldn't do anymore, another joined me. It was Bugs, his large front teeth and overbite just shining through the mud.

"Don't stare at the teeth. I can eat an apple through chain link fence. They call me Bugs," he said as he gritted out a pushup next to me. Now Bugs was here next to me in the mud, in the push-up position.

He looked over at me with those teeth showing and said, "Now why should I let you get all the credit for saving Ole Virgil."

I remember smiling, then wondering if Bugs was a little crazy. But it didn't matter if he was or not, I liked him. Bugs and I did push-ups and sit-ups in the mud for two more hours. The TAC said we were being punished for moving. The others had to join us. The others were being punished for not moving to help a fellow candidate.

Virgil quit two days later. He said he finally realized what was important in life. He was only there to impress his parents. And who knows, maybe Virgil saved his own life. Out of sixty candidates, only thirty-five graduated from the first phase of training. Bugs and I were among those. With our sweat and tears, we started our aviation careers in Fort Rucker, Alabama, and now we are here in Iraq together, once again in the dirt, only this time it's sand.

"It's good to see you, Bugs!" I said as I dropped my bags on a vacant cot.

"Yeah, yeah, Lanceford," he said, in a half mumble. He always called me Lanceford for some reason.

"So you made it, Luke! I've been flying with the lieutenant," Matt Benton said as he dropped a new map of Iraq on my bunk.

"You might want to dedicate this map to memory."

"Will know it in thirty-one-point-two seconds," I said with my usual reply.

Matt Benton would be my combat buddy, or the backseat pilot assigned to me. We would fly together the entire time for all combat missions. We would be everywhere the other was for the entire time we were here.

Bugs was assigned as a member of our troop and would fly as wingman for Matt and me.

Our home away from home was a concrete building that had been blown apart in Desert Storm. We simply washed it out with JP-4 Jet fuel, put a canvas tent over the top and moved in. It was good because of ballistic protection from small arms fire, and it was dark in the daytime so we could sleep for our night missions.

Just as I finished unpacking, Captain Johnson pulled the tent flap back. He had a flashlight in his hand and was wearing his kevlar helmet.

"Luke, get some sleep. You're going up on a recon in the morning with your buddy Matt," the Captain said as he welcomed me to Iraq.

Pulling the sleeping bag tight under my chin, I tried to get comfortable on the small metal and canvas cot. The night felt as restless as a hungry wild animal, and my body still seemed to vibrate with the blades of the helicopter. Somewhere between thoughts of the nightmare flight and my family three thousand miles away, I drifted off to sleep.

The morning sun was already above the distant mountains when I awoke. I squinted one eye while rubbing the other. Matt was already up, sitting on the edge of his cot, his dog tags hanging from his neck. He was dressed in gray shorts and a brown Army-issue T-shirt. He held one of the razors from the free gift packs in his right hand, a small mirror in his left.

"You ready?" he asked as he pulled the razor through the thick mounds of shaving cream.

I replied with a grin.

"Does that mean yes?" I give him thumbs up with a bigger grin.

But my grin faded as our day found us flying a recon mission just northeast of Dahok, Iraq. The stale smell of dirt and rot filled the cockpit as I brought the 17,000-pound helicopter to a hover over the remains of the Kurdish village. It was obvious from the large crater that this area had been bombed by artillery shells. Bodies lay frozen in time: women slumped over, clutching their young, and men face down in the dirt. The bodies were beginning to take on the blue tint of aged death. I was puzzled by the total lack of wounds. Everyone had just dropped in their steps. No guts and blood, just dead people. I reached for my chemical mask but suddenly remembered that the Army didn't issue us the Apache version of the flight mask, and the other mask wouldn't fit our sighting system.

"Let's get the hell out of here!" Matt said, as he radioed to Bugs, our wingman.

"I'm with you," I mumbled as I tried to hold back my breakfast.

I couldn't eat dinner that night. The next morning my stomach still wasn't in the mood; besides, the eggs we had for breakfast had a great resemblance in color to the dead villagers. So I passed on breakfast as well.

For several days I thought of the village. As for who or what killed the villagers, I'm not sure. But the image of it remains frozen in my memory, like those bodies were frozen in time. I would close my eyes to sleep, and there she'd be, dressed in that dusty old dress. Her back was against the mud hut and she was slumped down with her head tilted slightly to the right against her baby, a small human beginning to decay. The woman's face held a great sadness. I have often wondered if that sadness was from realizing her own death or that of her small child who had yet to know life.

It was my first week in Iraq and I already thought that the heat was starting to get to me and everyone else. We had only been there a few days, and it seemed like I couldn't even remember if there ever was another life....

CHAPTER FOUR
Another World

1991, Illeshiem Germany, My Wife and Kids.

A sharp whistle sliced through the morning. Her arm automatically reached for the alarm clock. With covers over her head, she slowly embraced the morning. As she pushed the covers down she realized she was in a strange place. As the seconds went by, the room became more and more familiar. Was it just a bad dream?

The whistle sounded again. Swinging her legs off the bed to land into two slippers, she made her way to the window.

"That German train, it always whistles," she thought as she ran her hand through her tangled blond hair and peered into the mirror on the dresser.

The image in the mirror just stares blankly: hair a mess, eyes puffy from too much sleep.

"What am I doing here?" she mumbled. Falling back on the bed for another minute of sleep, she heard the beat of small feet coming down the hall. The door opened and the bed is bombarded by a bright-eyed three-year-old.

"Get up mommy! Where is daddy? Is he still away?"

"Yes, he is." she said, looking over at the picture of a young army aviator next to the bed.

"That's my daddy; he flies helicopters!" the boy said as he pointed at the picture.

"Yes, he does. He sure as hell isn't here helping me with you and Ben!" she said out loud.

"He is in Iraq!" proclaimed the three-year-old.

"He's down there with the rest of the little boys, playing war," she said as she stood up, pulling on her robe.

"My daddy is fighting Saddam, mommy!" The little boy pointed a finger at his mother, now making her way out of the room to make breakfast.

"Well, hey there!" She stopped to greet her four-year-old son. He made a whining leave-me-alone noise.

A light steam rose from the coffee cup and brought a sweet aroma across her senses as she watched the two boys eat their breakfast.

"God, they look just like him," she thought.

"I could never leave." She sipped the coffee and thought back to those early days.

How did he ever make it to become an army pilot? I really never expected him to make it or I would have never agreed to go with him. All that flying stuff was just a dream. He was raised on a farm, for God's sake. This was never meant to be. Me, here in Germany waiting on a husband at war. How will I ever get my life back? Not to mention the two carbon copies I am mothering.

She took another sip. Letters, letters, all he ever wants is letters. I don't have time for letters. Plus there is nothing to say. I'm here, he's there, and life is the same as it was yesterday, as it was last month. Me here, washing clothes, cleaning house, washing dishes, and baby-sitting. What news should I write? "Dear you, this is me. I'm still here. Still here for you while you are living your dreams, while mine are on hold."

Love has its limits. I hope he is having fun, because I don't know how much longer I can handle these dreary overcast skies full of rain and snow. Not to mention the German way of life so different from the states. I sure hope he is having a good time.

Iraq

As quickly as the night left, the day brightened to 115 degrees, and in fourteen hours it would again fade to a 40-degree night. Here, a soaking wet towel would dry in fifteen minutes. A man must consume three liters of water a day or he would dehydrate and die. There were snakes, scorpions, and huge spiders. There were dust devil winds that could pick up cars and toss them like tin cans. There was sickness. Sickness everywhere. When it hit you, you would be dizzy, puke every five minutes, and poop all over yourself. You would have a fever of 104. You would freeze one minute and sweat the next. You would take IV's until you recovered. You would not care if you lived or died. You would pray to die. Then you would live.

The mess tent was next to the medical tent. So every morning we enjoyed our breakfast watching the sick soldiers throwing up next to us. And if that wasn't enough to make us want a second helping, we could always get a whiff of poop burning at the toilet tents. It seemed the Army in its infinite wisdom placed the medical tent and mess tent directly downwind of the poop tent.

"This is just great! People puking their guts out in front of me, and the fresh smell of burning crap in the air! Hell, we don' t need an enemy!" declared Bugs as he drops his plate down at the table.

Matt grabbed a plate. "Anyone want elegant dinning back in the comfort of our own homes?"

"Hell, that ain't no better. Besides it makes me hungry watching these guys puke!" Bugs said, talking with his mouth full of grits and eggs.

I decided to take my plate back to my bunk and eat there. After breakfast I looked over the mission brief for the night's mission. Laying my head back on my bunk and pushing my hat down over my eyes I begin to daydream back to my boyhood and my first days of flying.

My first flight 12 years old.

It was one month past my twelfth birthday at Rudy's Glider port, High Springs, Florida.

"Go ahead and climb in!" Rudy said as he tossed me a boat cushion.

"This should help you see over the dash." He chuckled as he finished the preflight of the blue and white Cessna 152.

The mere sight of all the dials and gauges was worth the week's pay. I sat forward and imagined myself as a fighter pilot awaiting a mission.

"This is awesome!" I thought out loud.

"That's what they all say," Rudy replied as he slid into the copilot seat next to me.

It would have taken surgery to remove the smile from my face on that day. Rudy took the controls and made everything look easy.

"These people want to learn flying, but never want to learn what makes the airplane fly," Rudy lectured as he maneuvered the Cessna to the runway for takeoff.

"You ready?" he asked, glancing over at me.

"Sure!" I answered with my eyes fixed on the runway in front of me.

"Okay, then take the controls," he said as he wiggled the fight controls.

"Sir?" I asked incredulously.

"Take the controls! You came to fly didn't you? You mean to tell me you want to pay forty dollars and not fly the airplane?"

If Rudy thinks I can fly, then I can! I thought, taking the controls.

"Put your left hand on the flight controls and your right hand on the throttle; the throttle gives the airplane power. Like this." Rudy demonstrated.

"Nothing to it!" he said with a big grin.

Hands on the controls like a veteran, I was ready.

"Now push the throttle forward, Okay, put both hands on the flight controls, look out ahead, and steer the airplane with the pedals."

The airplane was moving, slowly at first, then the speed increased. The grass on the runway was becoming a green blur.

"Now, just for a second, look at the airspeed indicator gauge." I looked down at the gauge Rudy was referring to. It read sixty knots.

"When that gauge reads sixty-five knots, start pulling back on the flight controls," Rudy ordered.

I glanced at the gauge. Sixty-two, three, four.

"Start easing it back," Rudy spoke as if he were talking to the airplane.

Just as he finished his words, the rough grass runway became really smooth. Too smooth.

I looked out the side window. I am flying! The little Cessna 152 hummed along as we flew north for about ten minutes. The air inside the airplane seemed cooler.

"So why do you want to fly?" Rudy asked as he pulled the throttled lever back bringing the little engine to a relaxed purr.

"I just love it," was the only response I could send across my lips.

For some reason the little aircraft was really bumpy. It was exciting to be flying, but something was not good. Suddenly something in my stomach was churning. I felt really hot. A tangy taste entered my mouth. I swallowed. The taste came back.

Rudy looked at me and reached behind the seat for a coffee can.

"Take this; it's a good place to put your lunch," Rudy said as he popped the top off the can.

Grabbing the can, I chucked up what was left of a hamburger. It smelled horrible. A mixture of cheese, bread soaked in stomach acid and cola. I thought I might be sick again.

"I think we've had about enough for today. There's not enough room in that can for my lunch, too." Rudy said, handing me a cloth to wipe my mouth.

Rudy landed the 152 and taxed to the hanger.

"Sure you want to fly?" he asked as he grabbed the coffee can from behind the seat.

I thought for about a half second.

"Sure I do! Will you let me go again next Sunday? I'll do my best to not throw up."

"Grab those cushions and be here next Sunday two o'clock sharp and we will punch another hole in the sky!" he said, walking to the hanger and looking over his shoulder.

The next three times I flew, I threw up, but with Rudy's patience and my consuming love for flying, somehow I made it to solo.

In those days flying was a dream. A simple dream paid for by pitching melons, bailing hay, and picking up eggs every summer and after school on the farm. The dream was practiced on Sunday afternoons with a teacher that knew how to help build dreams. With every flight there was more confidence. With confidence became an awareness of accomplishment. With an awareness of accomplishment became the belief that I could fly. I could be exactly what I wanted to be.

My thoughts grew into a belief that I had wings, then that belief grew feathers on those wings, and Rudy gently pushed me from the nest to became a pilot.

Now I was here on this bunk in Iraq. Ready. Ready for a sixteen-hundred-hour mission in the AH-64 Apache. I was amazed to think I really made it and so many others didn't.

I knew so many people that were a lot smarter than I was. I knew many people that were better pilots. But I never knew anyone that wanted this job more than I did. I guess that was the secret. I wanted it more and was willing to give it my all, anytime, just to be the one who was here.

"Get up, Luke! It's time to get the seal brief!" Matt called as he grabbed his kneeboard and headed out of the room.

I shuffled through my helmet bag, found my kneeboard, and followed Matt to the briefing tent. A dark-haired young man stood at a map. He was a little out of place because his hair was longer than ours, and he was dressed in a makeshift uniform to mimic the desert fighters of Iraq.

"This must be the seals," Matt whispered as the briefing began.

"The objective is here. The Apaches will hit here and here at 0300 hours. We will set a diversion here. Then the Hawks will insert blue team here and extract here. Time Hack is now 1100 hours. Any questions?"

"Ah, yes," Bugs raised his hand.

"Yes Mr. Hammock."

"Are we really going to be shooting or is this an exercise?"

"Life is an exercise, Mr. Hammock. You use real oxygen and real food, and you really live. Now here we use real ammo and real weapons, and you can really live or really die. So be ready. We don't like to think of this as real or not. All missions are real, even when we are practicing. Just think of us practicing on live targets that shoot back. Any more questions? Okay, gentlemen. Meet back here at 2100 for the final briefing."

And with that, the SEAL operator smiled and walked out. I noticed he had on the same watch I did. For some reason, I couldn't imagine this kid-looking soldier to be a soldier's soldier, a SEAL. In the movies they looked so mean. This guy seemed as nice as any common Joe.

For the mission, we were to destroy a convoy of tanks headed north, and the SEALs were to infiltrate the Iraqi underground caverns next to the Euphrates River. Our action would bring the focus of the Iraqi military to the tanks and away from our real intention: to control the Euphrates River from the unseen caves and caverns on the banks.

CHAPTER FIVE
The Valley of Death

Age 26, Somewhere in Iraq, 1991

I rolled and tumbled. The blazing desert sun mixed with sand and flies made it hard to sleep. A thin bug net hung between me and the vulturous flies. The hot wind left a fine cover of dust on everything in the tent, including me. I lay in my cot collecting my thoughts for the night's mission. A scorpion made its way out from under my cot, crawled across my pistol, up the strap of my gas mask, and onto the side of the tent.

Getting up and preparing to fly only required two legs in a flight suit, one zipper, and two boots laced. And if time allowed, washed face, brushed teeth and a shave.

The 2100 mission briefing was short and sweet. Much of the same ole same, a basic review of the SEAL briefing. The teams are divided, timelines set, frequencies given, weapons loads checked, and maps plotted.

Even though we have practiced this a thousand times, I knew this mission would be different. For the first time in my life I was going on a real mission... And there was a great chance that blood would be shed.

The desert-sand-colored Chevy pickup dropped us off at the aircraft. The crew chief was already there awaiting us. I walked around the aircraft one last time to assure myself that everything was closed and latched, then climbed into my appointed element-of-war. As I strapped on the shoulder harness, my crew chief climbed up on the side of the aircraft.

"What's up?" I asked.

"Well sir, I just wanted to say..." he hesitated.

"Spit it out," I said as I buckled the harness.

"Well, sir, all my life I have wanted to be a pilot, and I have always envied you guys getting to fly, but tonight I'm glad it's you going out there in the dark instead of me. I know you and Mr. Benton will make it. I believe in you, and I am praying for you." He shook my hand and climbed down before his eyes watered.

I smiled at him, then shut the canopy. Just before my mind settled into my mission I said a prayer. In less than a second I was clean and ready. Ready for whatever this night held for me.

Minutes later, the desert night echoed with the sound of a thousand locusts as our six AH-64 Apache attack helicopters roar across the God-forsaken terrain of Northern Iraq.

Matt, my back seater, advised me that we were approaching the border.

"Border five miles," Matt replied.

This was my cue to place the master arming switch to the arm position. As if preprogrammed, my left hand reached through the darkness, landing on the cold master arm peg. With a click, I noticed that the master arm light now glowed red, illuminating the left side of the fire control panel. This simply meant the aircraft armament was ready to fire.

As my left hand left the arm switch, it gave a slight swivel to the cockpit mirror so I could see Matt in the back seat. His ghostly looking helmet in the shadows of the back cockpit reminded me of an alien bug. Who would know, under all that, was Matt Benton, a mild-mannered husband and father, a former Eagle Scout and hall monitor, and a good friend to all. But on this day he was a U.S. army attack pilot and my battle buddy. Matt and I had been flying together for several months. He had a lovely wife that wrote him everyday. His little girl was only two years old, but always scribbled a picture on her mom's letters. He kept all of her little drawings in a ziplock bag in the left leg pocket of his flight suit. He said it brought him good luck. He was one of the best pilots I had ever flown with and it was good to be with him tonight.

My right hand, covered with the green and gray flight gloves, reached between my knees to grip the cyclic flight control. At the same time my left hand grabbed the collective flight control on the left side of the seat.

"I have the controls!" I announced to Matt.

"Roger, you have the controls!" He affirmed.

I felt the aircraft respond ever so slightly as I wiggled the controls. Other than a slight moon and a heavenly array of stars, the sky was dark. The light sand on the ground is brighter than tonight's sky.

"Okay, Luke, let's do it! Hope this baby works as advertised!"

Luke was my pilot name. Matt always called me Luke even when I visited with him at home. He said we were real Jedi knights.

The vibrations intensified through my armored seat as I pushed the controls to make the large wasp dive to the earth like a homesick anvil. Seconds later, ten feet off the ground, one hundred and forty knots, we blasted across the sand like the cavalry did long ago on horseback. As we flew lower, the ground became a mere blur from the speed.

"It will be a long walk back if anything happens!" blurts out the lieutenant over the secure line.

"You could ride a camel," Bugs answers.

"Does this area have one-hump or two-hump camels?" Matt added.

The other voices in my earphones were coming from the two helicopters in tight formation in front of me. We were flying so close that one slight mistake could result in one big fireball over the desert. Pieces of aircraft would be scattered for miles. When and if our bodies could be found, we would be shipped home in flag-draped boxes. If we weren't found, our dog tags would lie here in the sand forever.

My heart rate increased to offset the adrenaline pumping through my veins. The cockpit of this fourteen million dollar air machine was lit with a slight green glow from the instruments. It was cool inside from the A/C unit blasting arctic air into our plexiglas environments. Just outside my window hang eight hellfire missiles and seventy-two folding fin rockets, with enough explosives to destroy a convoy of tanks or small town.

"Weapons check?" called Matt.

I scanned my hands over the switches, checked the symbology projected in my Helmet Display Unit (HDU), which is mounted over my right eye. Everything looks right.

"Weapons check, good. Ready for bear!" I replied.

"Make your call, your two miles out, Matt answers.

I pressed the microphone trigger and spoke as if I was speaking to the divine.

"North Star, North Star, this is Bushwacker two-four. We are at red line requesting passage to crime scene."

North Star was an airborne radar plane that controlled the skies over Northern Iraq. The voice of North Star was that of a sexy- sounding lady with a northern accent.

"Bushwacker, you are cleared to pass red line and proceed as requested. Happy hunting!" the soft voice replied.

"Do you think she is as pretty as she sounds" asked Matt.

"She's probably big and fat, with freckles. But that's okay. After we stay here another six months I'll probably love to meet her," I added.

The Doppler Navigation System counted down to the checkpoint and began blinking.

The lead aircraft called,

"This is lead. Crime scene."

"Well, Toto, I don't think we're in Kansas anymore!" Bugs added one last bit of humor to loosen everyone's tension.

The closer we got to the enemy the more I realized time was the only thing that couldn't be bought. No matter how much money we have, it's the only factor between us and our destiny. It seemed like minutes, but we'd been flying for at least two hours. The joke about walking back now seemed to take on a different meaning. It was a ghostly feeling to know that if you went down here, everyone would be trying to kill you.

"Got us on the map?" Matt asked.

I glanced down at the glowing screen of the Doppler, then checked my knee board for distance and time.

"On course," I assured Matt.

"Just checking! You know the Donkey?" Matt always referred to the lieutenant as the Donkey. And on this night, the lieutenant was flying lead.

The helicopter gave a small shutter followed by a muffled rumbling sound, as we slowed to take position one hundred yards apart and in line with the other six Apaches.

We called set, having brought our war machines to a hover many miles from the enemy. The Iraqi tanks were on a road running north and south leading into the northern areas of Iraq. I remembered from our mission brief that the road itself was a hardtop with very soft sand on both sides. Our plan was to attack the enemy out of his weapon range and be a total surprise. If we could hit the first and the last tanks, then they would be trapped on the road.

My hands once again seemed preprogrammed as they moved in the pitch dark and placed all the right switches in the right positions. It was amazing how well pure repetition could help one perform in times of stress. I almost felt as if I was sitting back watching the army product perform.

My right eye was looking into the darkness through a FLIR, forward-looking infrared monocle. After a couple of hours of night flight with the monocle, my eye felt like I'd been looking into a flashlight. My left eye had no monocle but scanned the horizon for signs of visible light.

After a long nights mission this visual setup produced a splitting headache. The army considered night flying with the FLIR so stressful that it factored two hours of FLIR flying for every one hour actually flown. I wondered what the stress factor was for FLIR in combat.

Our Intel reported that the Iraqi tank crews had been traveling north for several days. Their bellies were probably grumbling from lack of food and their hearts aching for the loved ones they felt they were protecting. And I couldn't help wondering if any one of those tank crew members woke this morning thinking this would be his last.

Tonight they would never know what hit them. If they were lucky, they would see a small flash on the horizon. If not, their bodies would never be found among the debris of scrap metal, each headstone only a small pillar of black smoke in the morning sky.

It was only seconds now before we became the death angel. Emotions were locked out and stored away on some distant shelf in our minds. Matt and I settled into our bubbles and focused only on the mission. The tone of our voices transformed from the happy-go-lucky pilots into non-emotional grim reapers. Back home we were really nice guys, but at work we were who we were programmed to be. Our mothers wouldn't want to see us at work.

Our six Apaches slowly began to hover forward just fast enough to stay ahead of the dust cloud produced by our rotor blades. We were divided into three teams of two: red, white, and blue. The Lieutenant was lead and called the shots. Still out of the enemy's weapon range, we began the attack.

"Red team, this is lead. My spot is center. Yours is left. Blue team, you're right. All set?"

"Red set!" Bugs called.

"Blue set!" Matt called.

I scanned the enemy one last time and locked my line of sight on the last tank. Awaiting the word, my heart pounded. I had to remember to breathe.

"Northstar, this is bushwhacker element. We are set," called the lieutenant.

"Bushwacker, you're clear hot!" Northstar replied.

"That's their death sentence," Matt whispered into his voice-actuated microphone.

"You got a good target?" Matt asked.

"Target is one T-64 tank, last in formation. Weapons set, laser ready."

"On three—three, two, one…"

My finger flipped up the trigger guard, and landed on the forbidden live trigger spot. This was the point in practice where we stopped.

"Let 'er rip, Luke!" Matt's anxious reply cut through the static of my earphones.

"One hellfire, alpha code, left rail. Laser on, missile launch!" I called with the same program professional voice one would hear at Cape Kennedy during a rocket launch.

A bright flash filled the cockpit as the missile blasted into the night. At first, the flash startled me. But it seemed that the more I pulled the trigger, the better the flashes looked.

"It has begun!" Bugs called over the radio.

Systematically we began deleting the enemy. It was like a scene from a science fiction movie. With the infrared monocle covering my right eye, I zoomed in on my prey several miles away. With the slight turn of a knob in the dark, I focused my night vision system to positively identify another enemy tank. With a squeeze of the trigger

I sent another laser-guided hellfire missile. Another bright flash as the missile took flight and arched upward. I held my breath as I watched the screen over my right eye. From the top of the screen a small projectile appeared—it was the hellfire. A bright fireball filled the screen as the missile shattered the tank into a million pieces of molten metal. The bodies inside were instantly vaporized.

"Good shooting, Luke!" Matt shouted, having seen the shots on the video screen in the back cockpit.

Giving humanity one last chance, I paused a second to allow the crew members in the other tank an opportunity to realize their fate, open their hatches, and run to safety.

Just another trigger squeeze and the clock of death was once again ticking with the sound of loud blasts as 2.75 inch folding fin rockets left the wing pods and disappeared into the night. Seconds later the world lit up with a massive firestorm.

Through the night vision monocle, I could see images of bodies being blown in half while they were still standing, others running and burning. The lucky ones fell straight to their deaths.

Another click of a switch gave me a higher magnification of the area. As I scanned, looking for any possible armed foe, I became a witness to modern warfare. This was the part the video game didn't show.

My stomach turned as I witnessed the ghostly image of the final failure of humanity. A body lay blown in half, yet jerking and gasping from its last reflexes. I turned the video screen off.

The warm breath of the devil sent cold chills down my sweat-drenched back as I watched all this death around me. I could almost hear their souls crying out as Evil ran rapidly across the battlefield. Feeling its presence, I said a small prayer: God please be with me.

"Down to the right!" Bugs screamed.

I instantly swung my head, focused my right eye, and squeezed the trigger to the thirty-millimeter cannon. Flesh and metal were blasted into the air.

"Where did they come from?" I complained.

"Probably a recon vehicle. Don't worry, we won that one." Matt said.

"I never saw 'em!" I complained.

"And they never saw us!" Matt came back. He always had a way of putting bad things in a good prospective.

My gut ached to realize the politicians had failed to the point that I had to do what I never really wanted to do—my job. For some reason war never seemed so deadly before. At school and church war always sounded so heroic, but tonight it left the stench of death on my clothes. My heart said this wasn't good. Why is man so damn stupid? Why do we kill each other with little or no remorse? My God, what have we become?

"Animals!" The tent flap flew back. In walked the commander cursing and screaming about the mission.

"You are all animals and I love it! You kicked ass and didn't even want to take their names!"

I looked over at Matt. He adjusted his shorts, sat on the bunk and ran his fingers through his short black hair. The commander's loud mouth interrupted the card game already in progress over in the corner.

I pretended to continue to write. Matt pretended to straighten the pillow on his cot. The Commander started talking about an extension here for three more months. Matt glanced out from beneath knitted brows, shook his head and mumbled something that sounded really close to horse's ass. The Captain, who seemed to be the only one jumping for joy was already thinking of himself as a war hero and he wasn't even on the mission. Tonight the room grew somewhat quiet as the Captain carried on about the bad guys. As for me, I went back to writing. The other warrant went back to playing cards, pretending to ignore the Captain and pretending to ignore the fact we were over three thousand miles from the people we loved.

Same Night
Wife in Illeshiem, Germany

"Let's dance," he said.

She looks up at the young lieutenant. His black hair and Italian good looks were accentuated by his officer's uniform. He held out his hand.

She glanced back at her girlfriends at the table. They winked. She took his hand.

Iraq

My body was still vibrating from the night's mission and my head ached from wearing the night vision monocle. The mission was over.

Feeling homesick I tried my luck at the phone lines. After being in Iraq for two months the Army allowed us to use the remote satellite telephones to call home. The only problem, we were to share with everyone in Northern Iraq. The waiting lines were hours long.

Exhausted but restless, I stood in line, eyes wide, staring up at the stars twinkling like miniature diamonds on black velvet. For a moment I felt as if I could reach up and touch each and every one of them, but like the family I waited to talk to, I felt as though they are billions of miles away. Was there someone, somewhere out there on one of those twinkles in the same situation as I, at war in a foreign land? A small part of me hoped maybe whoever or whatever was out there had gone beyond war. Yes, maybe there was intelligent life out there after all, observing our sorry nature. For a moment I felt ashamed for us.

It was two a.m. on a Saturday night and I held my breath awaiting her voice. The phone rang and rang. No answer. I hung up and re-dialed. Still no answer. I hung up and went back to the tent.

Two days later I tried to call again. It was one thirty in the morning when I finally got the phone. This time I got her voice.

"Hello......hello," she said with a sleepy voice.

"Hey, honey! How are you doing? I'm not sure how long I will be able to talk so don't be mad if we get cut off."

"Why are you calling so late? I'm trying to sleep. Call me back at a better time."

My heart sank. She wasn't very excited to hear from me.

"How have you been?" I asked, trying to get her to talk.

"I've been. That's about it."

"What's wrong?" My heart was breaking. I could feel something really bad was wrong.

"Not much, but I better tell you before you hear it from your friends and wig out on me."

My body felt numb from her words. But I continued to listen.

"I've been out."

"Please, if what your about to say is bad."

"Listen, I've got to say this. I've been out. I was dancing and had a few drinks. And I met this guy. He doesn't mean anything to me."

"Please, whatever happened. Just forget it. Don't tell me."

In the movies when the actors hung up the phone there is a tone. In real life there is nothing. Three weeks later I received a large yellow envelope. There was no good-bye letter or even a note. Just some fancy wording done by a lawyer. The message was clear—bye.

My footprints led back to the tent. I brushed the dust off of my bunk and unrolled my sleeping bag. The other Warrants were sleeping. I laid my head on the pillow and wondered how. But I knew it wasn't a big mystery. It had been coming across the field of my life like a bullet fired from a gun. Right on time to hit me here at this time and place, giving me no option but to accept the wound. I knew that by choosing this life, this wounding was inevitable. At times I tried to prepare myself, but when it hit, it still almost killed me.

Her memories, our memories stored away and locked. The key now sat on a dusty table in the back corner of my mind. I tried to sleep. I tumbled and tossed in the three-foot- wide bunk, but my mind kept playing the scenes from my family.

The day I left for Iraq. She had really loved me at one time, or had she? I replayed the day frame by frame, trying to find some sort of hint. The parking lot that day was full of good-byes and tears as we all said our parting words to the ones we loved.

Like a scene from a movie, she gazed deep into my eyes and said, "I love you, and I will be here when you get back." Big tears slowly made trails down the sides of her young face as the words seemed to cause her more pain. I knew this scene all too well, for I had rehearsed it in my mind since the orders came. What would I do? Could I leave and go fight for this country, this president, or whatever the reason. Would I take someone's life? Would I fail in the heat of battle? Would I still know this beautiful woman I called my wife? Will she still know me? Will she still love me? What will I learn? What will I lose? All these questions raced through my mind as the lump grew in my throat. My three children held to my legs for dear life.

"Where are you going daddy?" their little innocent voices pleaded for answers to why their lives were being thrown into turmoil.

Their little faces were so full of life. I held back my tears trying to look them in the eye and give them reassuring answers. But the words were somehow taken away by the large pain in my heart.

With my bags in hand, I leaned over to give my three little ones a big hug and kiss, then turned and walked away with only one last look back at three sad faces. Their little hands gave a slight wave good-bye. That was the last time I knew my family.

Just as my thoughts begin to turn to dreams, and snores echoed across the tent it hit. Bam! Bam! The ground shook so hard I thought the tent would fall. Bam! Bam! What in the world!

Waking fast, mind running the rpm's, trying to remember what to do in an attack.

"Gas mask!" screamed someone.

I felt around in the dark for my gas mask, hands shaking and mind racing. Adrenaline hit my blood stream: nine seconds to put on mask, do it, do it now, live, breath, calm down. Mask in place, breathing clean air. Stomach aching from hitting the floor so hard. I ran the totals: clean air, check; stomachache, no big deal; pistol, in hand; blood, none; final total, everything good.

I looked around in the dark. Figures were running in and out of the building. I heard the sound of gunfire in the distance, heavy gunfire, at least a fifty-caliber machine gun. There was a large explosion, then another. Then silence. Total silence.

One hour later and still silent, but I could hear the whispers of the wind. And then I remembered, they never issued us any bullets. More silence. I could hear myself swallow. My stomach growled.

"Hey, Luke! Wake up!" the lieutenant said.

I looked around and realized I had fallen asleep in my gas mask with my pistol in my hand. My lungs were sore from sleeping in my gas mask.

"What happened?" I asked.

"Just a terrorist firing mortars. The 50 hit him. Mortars aren't usually accurate." said the lieutenant.

"Tell that to all those who died in mortar attacks in Vietnam," said Mitch Reaves.

"Yeah, Luke, the mortars aren't accurate till they hit us." Bugs said.

"But it still was scary as hell!" added Matt.

The Captain walked in and announced,

"Congratulations, gentlemen. We are not flying for three days".

The sun was burning outside. My body started to take on a two-day stink. It occurred to me that the MRE's (meals ready to eat) had clogged my system and made my stomach ache. So I decided to make a journey of forty steps to the outhouse tent.

Pushing back the tent flap, the smell hit my nose about the same time the flies flew toward my mouth. I spit at the flies and gagged at the smell. The tent was arranged with a plywood shelf on each side with round holes cut as a makeshift toilets. Of course there was no privacy. One could sit next to someone and stare across the tent at someone else with diarrhea. The flies loved this place. They would fly down and land on the poop, fly up and land on your exposed butt, then circle the tent and land back in your face. Someone once told me that you could always tell what type of place you're at by the restrooms. Well, if that is so, then we were somewhere west of hell!

Being the clean freak, I decided to take a shower after my trip to the poop tent. I found my black five-gallon water can, which was nice and warm from the desert sun. Behind three pieces of plywood, our shower was a small bucket on a string attached to a small pulley for hoisting the bucket over your head. I dumped a little water over my head, then applied soap, and dumped the rest of water to rinse.

The uniform of the day when not flying was shorts, t-shirt, and boonie hat. The flight suit was simply too hot, and we only had three, so keeping them clean was important. The game was always volleyball. We played more volleyball than is played at Daytona Beach. The Navy Seals could always find a good beating here at B-troop. We were the East Hell volleyball champs.

CHAPTER SIX
Generations

The old men. That's what we called the old Warrant Officers W4's. The ones that had been in the Army for 20 years or more. Like John Conners.

John was always telling us the lessons of Vietnam, but none of the lieutenants or captains would listen. It was sort of funny how he would always end up right.

John always sat and smoked cigarettes with Bob Beachum. John and Bob were the old men. I didn't smoke; none of the new warrants smoked. We were the new improved version of Bob and John. We were more fit, blind followers, and eager to die if necessary. Bob and John were laid back. They had been flying helicopters so long that flying was easier than walking for them. We would sit and listen to them for hours.

"Luke, you know all this is a bunch of bull, don't you?" John said.

"What are you talking about?" I asked.

"This war... hell, this crap has been going on for thousands of years. We will be here for six months to a year. Then the army will be right back here in ten years to fight these same people again."

"Do you think so?"

"I'm sure of it! Those damn politicians don't have the balls, and the American public doesn't have the stomach to really fight and finish a war. Just like Vietnam. The war went great 'til the politicians wanted to fight a *humane* war, holding back on bombing the population. See, it's the population that allows these dictators. Don't think for one minute that some sweet Iraqi mother of four wouldn't hand them the knife to cut your head off. What is the difference between a soldier and a civilian? Simply a uniform and the resolve to fight. Take away a uniform and any civilian in a blink of an eye can be a soldier. So don't trust anyone here that is Iraqi.

"And the Syrians and Iranians will be sticking their noses in here before it's over. Hell, the Syrians are more of a problem then the Iraqis. The Syrians are just snakes in the grass. You stay in the special ops community long enough and you will eventually see some Syrian or Iranian connection to a target you are shooting at. The politicians are simply ignoring the real problem, and that is Muslim extremists. If they attacked the real problem we would be hitting Syria and Iran tonight. That would be a good start if they were serious about solving this problem. And I don't mean surgical strikes. I mean carpet-bombing cities. Get the attention of the rest of the world that we mean business. Just like Vietnam, if we would have bombed the hell out of North Vietnam everyday with B-52's, then that war would be in the win column. Truman was the only president with the guts to make the hard decision to win a war. Ever since then we have been simply fighting wars, not winning them."

"Sounds like you got it figured out," I said as I contemplated the Syrian border only five miles south.

"Hey, how do you think us old men are old men?"

"Hope you wrong." I said.

"If we are back here in ten years, then we were right. If not, then we were wrong." John said before he took another draw from his cigarette.

"And you will see this for yourself," said Bob.

"I won't, I'm getting out after this one!" I said.

"Getting out?" asked Bob.

"Yep," I replied with a nod.

Bob Beachum lit a cigarette took a long draw, blew out the smoke and said,

"Let me let you young bucks in on a little secret. Most that get out come back in because there is no place in the civilian world for an attack pilot. You're no exception. Apache pilots are like all other attack pilots. We roam the battlefield seeing everything through the crosshairs of vigilance. Compartmental organizers with a sort of controlled recklessness, snapped to form by shear irrational logic. We only find comfort at the extreme edge of stress. And that stress eventually stretches to insanity. And insanity being the final resting place for those of us that survive the rest that found an honorable glorious exit from this sickness we all possess."

I just sat and listened as Bugs took a drink from his liter water bottle.

"You boys can't make it out there in civilian life. Or maybe I should say the civilians can't handle you. You're a different breed. There are two types of people in this world: desk clerks and fighter pilots. You are a fighter pilot, excuse me, an Apache pilot. You don't have a choice; it's the way you are made. You would die in the cage of civilian life or go crazy."

I thought about that for a minute.

Bugs said, "Bullshit! I can do anything! Hell, I was chosen over a thousand men for this position! We had to have something special."

And then John Conners jumped in,

"You think you have something special, you're right, but it ain't the highly intelligent boy scout they are looking for. Maybe that's the outside wrapper, but inside they want guys who are extremely confident and crazy as hell. The kind who feel the rush to climb the fence, sneak in and paint the school bleachers with spray cans, that's really us. The Apache pilots of today."

"I ain't never sprayed bleachers!" Bugs said indignantly.

John crushed out his cigarette with his boot and continued, "Think about it. Who is crazy enough to fly 140 knots, ten feet off the ground, two hundred miles behind enemy lines in the dark, through the Soviet's best air defenses and believe you cannot get hit or die? Just because we are better than everybody else? Look in the mirror Buck Rogers! It's the confident crazy ones they are looking for, and you were picked from over one thousand other crazy ones."

Bugs looked at John then at Bob.

Tim Johnson, Bug's back seater walked up as John was finishing his sentence to tell Bugs they had a flight to make. Bugs stood up, grabbed his hat and started to walk off. He stopped, turned around and said, "We are crazy, but damn proud of it!" He flashed us a grin as he left.

For some reason I knew the old men were right. We were definitely crazy. I remember drag racing on Friday and Saturday night. Running from the local cops. Always pushing things to the stress point. Somehow spending my time while monitoring the RPM gauge of my life, just waiting to shift to the next stressful event just at the precise moment not to over rev on any particular event. Viewing everything through some sort of crosshairs carefully calculating a sure route to victory, no matter what the event or situation. Maybe it was born in us. I couldn't remember ever not being this way.

As the old men talked, I could hear their voices in the back of my mind, but my eyes were watching a Dutch helicopter land. The blades slowed from a blur to a slow turn, then stopped.

At first I thought it was a mirage, or that I was seeing things. No it was a woman. It had better be anyway. Those curves, the long black hair, it was for sure a woman. She took off her helmet and shook out her long black hair. Maybe it was the heat affecting my vision. No it was definitely a woman. She walked across the camp from the helicopter, as heads began to turn and follow her well-curved flight suit. I was fully aware of my stare. My eyes were enjoying those nice curves and shining black hair as much as any red-blooded male who had not seen this type of beauty for about four months.

Her path was straight past our tent. As she approached, I acted as if I did not see her. Her footsteps were closer, and I looked up. As our eyes met, I saw a dark tan face with soft features. But those eyes shot through me to land somewhere in the back of my vision. We continued to stare at one another as she moved closer.

"Good afternoon," I said, trying not to stare.

"For you and me it is," she said. I heard the European accent.

She never slowed her walk, passing by as she spoke and looking once over her shoulder with a slight smile.

At that moment I noticed her lips, smooth and perfect as they made a smile.

I spent the rest of the afternoon washing my flight suit in a pan and writing in my spiral notebook.

I wrote: *Today I forgot Linda for a few minutes. Maybe there is hope.*

The next day I noted the time the Dutch helicopter landed. On schedule. Kicking up dust as it settled next to our camp. My eyes waited. Long black hair from under the helmet, curves pushing on the flight suit in places that demanded attention from any man, that regal princess walk. Closer, closer, now the eyes. Hazel in color and beautiful.

Her eyes were searching our camp. I settled myself in a lawn chair, four feet from where I was sure she would be walking. My boonie hat was pulled down close so she would not notice me until she was about ten feet away.

Her eyes were still searching. Who was she looking for? Her eyes focused on her path, then up to the book

I was holding. Our eyes locked once more. This time she stared, then looks away, only to look back deep into my eyes, maybe even into my soul, never breaking her stride.

I felt small tingles in my stomach.

"Is this all you American pilots do, sit and read?" she asked.

"Except when we are rescuing our ally's pilots," I replied with a little arrogance.

"So you would rescue me? Hmm, that would be interesting, now wouldn't it? It seems to me the Apaches break more than the Allouettes." Those lips spoke with the perfect accent. She reminded me of a James Bond woman.

"How long have you been flying Allouettes?" I asked, noticing her patch on her right shoulder that showed one thousand hours of Allouette time.

"Nice patch," I said.

"Well earned, that one," she replied. "I have been flying for about five years now. And you?"

"Three years for the Army, and since I was twelve in the real world," I answered, focusing again on those beautiful eyes.

"How is the war treating you?" she asked, glancing down at the spiral notebook I was holding.

"It treats me. Actually today is my birthday. I am officially twenty-six years old," I said with a big smile.

"You're kidding me! Well, I'm sorry you must have a birthday in this Godforsaken place, but you must have a cake or gift or something to celebrate."

"No, and don't say it too loud or the guys will think up some sort of practical joke to pull," I said with my finger over my mouth.

"Well, we Dutch take birthdays seriously. Yours will be no different. I will be back shortly."

With that she turned headed toward the Dutch area of the camp.

I wondered what in the world she was about to do. Visions of twenty Dutch marines singing happy birthday to me was a little scary.

The afternoon passed with no sign of the Dutch pilot. Just as I was reclining on my bunk to study some maps, Matt called out.

"Luke! There's a woman out here to see you."

Oh, my gosh, it must be her! What in the world is she up to?

I walked out of the tent to see her smiling, standing there with a little piece of cake with one candle and a birthday card.

"Where did you find that?" I asked, my mouth opened in surprise.

We were over a thousand miles from the nearest Coke machine and she found a cake, a candle, and a card. The Dutch did have their stuff together.

"Let's just say the Dutch are always prepared!" she said with a permanent smile.

"Although we don't sing as much as the French, we do hold birthdays in high regards!"

"Wow, thanks!"

"Your are quite welcome. If you would like, you can come to our camp tomorrow and see our operations tent. There are a few pilots you might like to meet."

"Sure!" I said.

"Be here tomorrow at this time and we'll fly to Silopy."

"Ten-four!" I replied with a grin.

Returning to the tent, I took out a Meal Ready To Eat or MRE, and a liter of water, sitting both beside the cake.

Birthday number twenty-six. What a place to have a birthday! I could really have used a dinner at Red Lobster!

I began to eat the MRE, imagining it was a feast, and thinking about birthdays.

Birthdays are special only when you're young. When I was sixteen, my birthday flight was almost my last. I was judged that day and was found untrained. I was a new pilot with no limits and in June of 1982, I was tested.

Age 16, Rudy's Gliderport, High Springs, Florida.

My third solo flight. My confidence was at its peak as I climbed into the cockpit of the small blue and white Cessna 152 aircraft. Other than the butterflies in my stomach, I was ready to go.

I flipped all the necessary switches to their starting positions and yelled "clear" out of the window. I turned the key and the engine sputtered to life. I moved down the check list, diligently calling each step out loud:

"Radios on, check: flight instruments adjusted, check."

On this day I was pilot and copilot. Dressed in blue jeans, tee-shirt and a grin from ear to ear.

Checks completed, I taxied the little plane to the runway, made a radio call to any other aircraft in the local area, and turned the nose of the plane to line up with the runway.

For some reason, there was an odd feeling in my gut, and a small voice said, "Pay attention to everything!" I almost stopped right there and went back, but my pride kept me on the runway. I checked every instrument twice, said a small prayer, and pushed the throttle to the fire-wall.

The aircraft rocked forward as I released the brakes. The grass runway was rough at first, but as the airspeed reached sixty-five, I pulled back on the flight controls and floated into the Florida sky. The steady hum of the

Lycoming engine gave me a warm feeling of security during takeoff. With fifty-foot trees on both sides of the runway, it was critical for the engine not to fail during takeoff. My eyes watched the ground slowly dropping away under the wheels of the aircraft. The engine purred, the gauges all in the green. The altimeter indicated I was now four hundred feet above the trees. All was well. Then it happened. The vibrations from the steady purring engine skipped. I froze. It skipped once more, then quit. I wanted to pass out. This could not be happening to me. My internal clock began ticking as my conscious counted down.

"You now have a maximum of twenty seconds to save your own life!"

My face felt hot, sweat started to run down my back. Then suddenly I lost all emotion, as if a switch had been thrown. Death was in my immediate future, but not without a fight.

"Fifteen seconds". The voice replayed in my mind.

The airspeed indicator read 65 knots. Just a half a second before, it had read 70 knots. I fought panic. I knew if the airspeed fell below 58 knots, this airplane would stall and there would not be enough altitude to recover before I impacted the ground.

The only thing that would bring the airspeed back was to lower the nose or add power. Since the engine was out,

I lowered the nose. I heard only wind noise as I lowered the nose. The noise and airspeed increased. The airspeed indicator needle bounced up to 65 then 70, the altitude needle slowly wound to 350. My choices were limited. I could land straight ahead in the woods or turn around and hit the runway I just took off from. Without further hesitation, I made a 180-degree turn for the runway. The turn took forever. Seconds seemed like hours. The aircraft slowed to 60 knots in the turn.

When I rolled out of the turn, wings level, the altimeter read 100 feet. The stall horn began to buzz. This meant the aircraft was about to drop below the speed it took to fly. Then it would fall uncontrolled from the sky.

There wasn't much sky left. I wasn't even sure the wheels would clear the trees.

The stall horn buzzed as the Cessna's wheels brushed the tops of the large live oak trees at the end of the runway. It sounded like a cat clawing on the bottom of the aircraft. Then the clawing stopped. Was I falling or flying? The stall horn was screaming. Sweat was making large trails down the side of my face. The runway rushed up to meet me. I pulled back on the controls and felt the tires touch the rough grass runway. I was down. Safe. I let out a deep breath as the aircraft rolled to a stop. This was my first encounter with the other side of flying. Rudy, my flight instructor, always said there was a wall in the sky, and that wall had two sides. One side, you're alive; the other side is the unknown." Today I was still alive. With every birthday we gain experience. I took another bite from the MRE. It was really difficult to imagine my cold chicken pack to be lobster.

CHAPTER SEVEN
Operators

The helicopter rocked slightly in the darkness as R.T. Bullock stared down the special night-vision range-finding scope. His right index finger rested outside the trigger well of the Remington rifle as he scanned the Iraqi camp for his target.

Stillness and calm. The crosshairs rose and fell with each breath. He was not calm enough and sought to find the stillness within. To find the bubble, crawl in, and lock the outside world away.

The crosshairs moved across the camp and settled on a second-floor window of a block building approximately eight hundred yards away. His index finger touched the button on the right side of the trigger well. The range flashed inside the scope, affirming 825 yards.

Inside the room sat a young man dressed in a light tan shirt and smoking a cigar. This man was the second in command of the Pershmerger rebels of Northern Iraq. He was responsible for planning attacks in Turkey and on the American bases in Iraq. He was most likely paid by Saddam to cause problems.

R.T.'s index finger moved to touch the trigger, while 120 miles away on a T.V monitor, a special operations commander saw the same image that R.T. saw through his rifle scope. If R.T. put his finger in the triggerwell he might see a red light inside his scope, meaning permission had not been given to make the shot. Tonight the light inside the scope was green. R.T.'s finger slowly squeezed the trigger. The sound of the round leaving the rifle is muffled by the helicopter. 825 yards away, the man's head exploded as his body crumpled on the floor. The others in the room froze in terror.

R.T. extracted the spent shell, catching it with his gloved hand, and chambered another all in one movement. He never took his eye from the target. The helicopter dipped its nose and began to disappear into the night.

Just as the helicopter picked up speed, a bright flash lit up the cockpit and sparks flew in all directions. The helicopter lunged forward, nose down, as the main rotor made contact with a large cable. Only twenty feet from the ground, the helicopter hit on its side, sliding into the Iraqi complex and coming to a rest only 200 yards from the block building which only minutes before had been the target.

R.T. crawled out of the OH-58 helicopter. He stopped to check the pilot's pulse. "Good, strong pulse. He was unconscious but alive. No fire, don't move till medivac could check his back," R.T. thought.

Priority one, secure this site! R.T. pulled out a small transmitter and pressed three buttons to send an SOS signal to special operations command in Silopy. This signal would alert the QRF Apache Helicopters and a SEAL rescue team. They would be in the Air in five minutes and on site in fifteen minutes.

R.T. grabbed his rifle and scanned the area. Six men were running in his direction 250 yards away. Crosshairs fell across the forehead of the man with the automatic rifle in hand. R.T.'s rifle jerked against his shoulder as the 308 bullet impacted the man's eye socket. He fell. R.T. swung the cross-hairs across the remaining men running in his direction to prioritize the next greatest threat. Crosshairs fell across the man screaming into his radio. The bullet slammed into the man's face just above his mouth, making him fall face first into the sand.

The next target was running faster than the others, but his chest exploded with a crimson mist of blood as the 308 bullet lifted him off his feet and dropped him on his back, not to move again.

Three to go. Running, another jerk of the 308 rifle, another man slid headlong into the dirt. Two more, 50 yards, R.T. pulled his H&K 45 pistol from his side holster and fired two rounds into both of the remaining men, so fast that they fell together, one overlapping the other. R.T. reholstered his 45 as he scanned the compound for any other enemy.

As we arrived over the compound, I could see a lone figure standing next to the crashed OH 58. I recognized R.T., one of the Seal snipers. He climbed into the rescue helicopter along with the injured pilot as we took over watching positions.

He simply said, "This area is secure," then sat against the bulkhead of the black hawk helicopter, rifle across his lap.

For R.T. Bullock this was just another mission. But for me, a young first-time-at-war pilot, this was a profound mission. I became aware of the other warriors in this war much closer to the fighting than I was.

Killing, it was all killing. Apaches at five miles or SEALs doing it with a knife up close, blood turned to brown stains in the sand only to be kicked to dust by the next boots.

I tried to relax in my bunk after this mission. Pulling out my 9mm pistol, I held it as I drifted off to sleep, wondering if this base was really secure and if all the avenues of approach had been thought of by security. Would I wake to a gun shot to the chest or a mortar exploding in my tent? Berretta tight in my grip, my left hand found the gas mask in the dark. No sheep to count, just ways the enemy could enter this camp.

Across the tent city in Silopy, R.T. Bullock cleaned his 45. He wiped it with an old rag, leaving hardly any oil residue to prevent the collection of dust or sand. He then cleaned his rifle with a barrel-brush, removing all the copper from the bullets fired earlier in the night. R.T. thought of his shots: not bad, sloppy in the chest, could have been a problem if his enemy had worn body armor. Next time, all head shots.

R.T.'s father left when he was young leaving R.T. to be raised by his mother and grandfather. His mother spent most of the time at work while R.T. spent most days squirrel hunting with his grandfather. One afternoon, his mother left with a man she had meet at work. She never came home. R.T. always wondered why. His grandfather died shortly after he graduated from high school, so R.T. joined the navy to do more hunting. Once in a while R.T. thought of his mother, but concentrated on teaching himself not to care. No wife. No time for a wife or family life with the operational tempo of the special operations community. The teams on the next mission were his family, the only family R.T. knew. As for the killing, no pleasure, no remorse, simply mission accomplishment at all cost. Never quit until the game is over. As for religion, R.T. believed that warriors didn't really die. They evolved to the next life and were once again warriors. From the first battles fought, to the Greeks, to the Romans, WWI, WWII, Vietnam, and now in this place in the desert in 1991. No matter what war or what cause, warriors always rose to the occasion.

R.T. finished cleaning his weapons and laid down on his bunk. The rest of the team was already asleep. R.T.'s right hand reached under his bunk for his 45 pistol. Holding it tight in hand, he went to sleep, thinking of a girl he had met in San Diego last year.

CHAPTER EIGHT
Mirage

Alexandria Orth joined the Royal Netherlands Air Force in 1986. She was one of the first women to fly helicopters. Raised in Holland in a port town, she spent much of her time sailing in her dad's 20-foot sailboat. She loved the feeling of freedom on the water. She found that same freedom in flying.

Having had a serious relationship years ago that left her feeling empty and betrayed, she put her career ahead of any relationship now. Knowing there was always time for family when she was too old to fly, she knew now was the time to live life luggage-free. Soon after flight school she was selected to fly the Allouette III. Men in the air force were simply too close to form any kind of relationship with. Alex knew men talked, and talk made women cheap. She was determined not to be cheap. However, late at night in her tent she would think of meeting someone special one day and finally trying to experience love. Alex knew that love, family, and men, would surely end her air force career in flying. She would get pregnant and be assigned to some boring desk, buried in paperwork. She had always thought never, until now.

Now there was that American pilot. He seemed distant, but close. Especially the way he looked her in the eye. This was going to be difficult, she thought. Maybe she should simply not talk to him again. Simply do her job and get home.

But why not? It never hurt to befriend an American. Beside she was long overdue for male company. It would also help the Dutch pilots to forget about the lesbian rumor.

"She never dates, she must like girls," they'd whisper.

Men--simple creatures. Always looking for something fast: fast planes, fast woman, fast cars, fast food, fast… Alex was not fast to follow some trail that led to heartache and the end of her career. So let them talk.

"So here I am!" Alexandria said.

"Let's go fly!" I said with my helmet in my hand.

We climbed into the Allouette III. It was a different helicopter. Everything was much older than our Apaches. Even the rotor blades turned differently. Our Apache blades turned counter clockwise. The Allouette blades turned clockwise, making all the controls move in reverse to compensate for the torque.

"Hold on, these birds are a bit rough on take off!" she said as she lifted the little helicopter off the ground, dipping the nose to pick up speed.

Dust blew away and swirled behind us as our forward airspeed increased. I recognized that Alex was a good pilot, smooth on the controls and mentally ahead of the aircraft.

"Would you like to go take a swim with the marines?" Alex asked.

I looked over at her to see if she was serious. She smiled with a slight grin. She was serious.

"Sure!" I said.

Alex rolled the aircraft to the right and dropped down to 100 feet, skimming the tops of the hills. The Dutch marines were camped on the banks of a small river that ran into the Euphrates. We circled their camp and lowered down to a small clearing next to the camp.

To my surprise, Alex climbed out of the helicopter and began to remove her flight suit, showing a black one-piece swimsuit. She threw me a pair of swim shorts and said, "Get dressed!"

She spoke in Dutch to the marines and they came over to welcome me.

Alex threw one marine her MP5 submachine gun and said, "Watch our six, mate."

"Don't worry, we have you covered with the 50-cal while you swim," the marine said.

"Shall we?" said Alex and turned and jumped into the river.

I looked at the marine, shrugged my shoulders and said, "I guess the lady is on point!"

I then jumped into her wake.

The river was very refreshing compared to the daily 120-degree temps. We swam for about fifteen minutes and then put on our flight suits and headed back to Silopy.

Alex was a different type of woman, fearless and sensitive at the same time.

"Did you have fun?" she asked.

"For the first time since I arrived here, I had fun!" I said, looking over at her as she began the approach into Silopy.

"This will be our secret. We can go again and there are some other neat places here in Iraq. I will show you."

She eased the cyclic back, slowing the helicopter over the pad, then gently set it down. As I climbed out, I could see Matt coming across the field to get me in the Chevy pickup.

"What's up?" I asked him.

"Get in, we have a mission!" he said.

One hundred miles away six British Special Air Service operators low crawled down the side of a block wall on the west side of one of Saddam's North palaces. The British had decided to get into a firefight with Saddam's guards.

The firefight had turned into a full shootout and the regular soldiers were pinned down. They called the SAS or the Brits' best, the Special Air Service. As the SAS soldier arrived at the end of the wall, he lobbed a grenade over, and awaited the blast. When it occurred, the other five SAS soldiers entered the courtyard, firing their Submachine guns. Each soldier hit a different Iraqi guard. Just that easy, it was over.

After the swim, the Apache seat was hot, and I was once again glazed with sweat from the heat. Matt powered the APU, and I began putting in coordinates to the palace. The report was that some British soldiers were shooting it out with the Republican Guard and requesting air support.

With both engines at flight speed, I lifted slightly on the collective. My view out of the windscreen was completely obscured by the sand. Brown-out we called it. I held the controls in a climb attitude, and the dust disappeared as the Apache began to outrun the dirt blowing into the air.

Matt calls Northstar, "Northstar, this is Bushwacker, up, inbound."

"You're clear!" Northstar answered.

I began to arm the aircraft when I noticed Bugs and Mitch pull up to our right side in chock 2.

"Two is up!" Bugs said.

"Roger Two!" Matt answers.

We lowered the noses of both Apaches to gain speed. All we knew was that the Brits were waiting and needed our help.

As we arrived at the palace, we called the Brits on the ground frequency.

"Red coat, this is Bushwacker, ready for metal!" I called.

"Bushwacker, redcoat, we are at index… repeat, index. Come on down and have some rum."

What? I rolled the aircraft on its side as we made a pass over the palace. The British flag was flying up the flag pole! British soldiers were swimming in the pool, waving at us. They had already killed the Iraqis and were now living it up at the palace.

I rocked my wings, rolling in tight then rolled out heading home.

Bugs crossed over my path behind me, almost taking the roof off of the palace. He rolled in tight on my right wing.

"Bloody Brits!" Bugs said.

CHAPTER NINE
Silence

Fifty thousand Kurdish refugees were displaced from their homes by Iraqi forces in Northern Iraq. Thousands of children were homeless and parentless. They were everywhere, these children without parents who either fled or were killed by Saddam's soldiers.

The army way was to stay in shape whether at war or in peacetime. So three days a week, I would run two miles. Since our camp was about one mile around the circumference, it only took two laps and my physical training, "PT", was done. The Navy Seebee's had pushed a large mound of dirt around our camp for protection from sniper fire. I would run inside of this mound.

Shorts, tee-shirt, and one small swig of water and I was off on a seven-minute-mile pace. My heartbeat increased with the steady pounding of my feet against the brown sand. The smell of burnt trash filled my lungs with every breath. The sky was always a deep blue, except when in bad weather when it turned dark brown. Today it was blue. As I made my way around the second turn, I noticed a dozier pushing up a pile of trash. The trash looked like hundreds of bags. The closer I got to the site, my lungs caught an odor that overpowered the burnt trash smell. Garbage? No, oh, no, it wasn't bags I saw, it was bodies! The dozier was unearthing a mass grave!

I stopped running, and began to gag. I looked away, only to look back once. I walked back to the camp, wondering why, what were the crimes that many could have committed all at one time.

Saddam was right, he didn't have any enemies in Iraq, they were all dead. If he once had enemies in this area, now only their sons and daughters remain, and they are clinging to the mountains, starving.

The old men, Bob and John, sat smoking outside the tent. As I approached, sweaty from my run and sick at heart from the site of the grave, I decided not to bring them down by relating the horror I had seen. I just asked if they had heard about the mass grave. That was it.

Bugs, Matt, Mitch, the lieutenant and I decided to find some way to make life better by cooling our tents. Green tents in the desert sun are hot, really hot. Matt had the idea of using some white packing tarps over the green. It worked; our tents were twenty degree cooler.

"The army hasn't changed a bit!" John said.

"These are the same kind of tents we had in Vietnam." Bob added.

Not long after we put the white top on our tents, the air force showed up with air-conditioned tents! I could never understand it. Here we were Apache pilots flying night missions in million-dollar aircraft who needed to sleep in the day in order to fly at night and we were issued worn-out GP medium tents that were hot, dusty, and allowed more flies than a syrup factory. Yet the air force privates enjoyed air-conditioned tents, free of flies. I guess we weren't supposed to apply logic. The question of the day and everyday was when were going home. We were told before our deployment this would be a three-month tour at most. Now after four months and no end in sight, we were all getting a little weary. Not that four months was unbearable, but we would have appreciated a straight answer.

Straight answers were hard to find anywhere here. Even from my own mind. Get ready, stand down, pack up, unpack. Plan a contingent for every mission; plan a backup for the backup. Rewrite you mission, get up, get down. My mind locked onto missions and ideas only to erase and redraw. My mind raced and idled, raced and idled. Flashes of children begging at the gates, of starvation, of arms and legs sticking out of the dirt. I imagined the sounds of blades turning in the distance. Gunfire and the smell of burnt plastic drifted in and out of my mind. The dead woman holding the dead baby. Dust, sand, death. My heart raced, so I took a deep breath and slowly exhaled, and again. I looked over at the SEALS tent. A man sat out under the awning staring across at the mountains and smoking a cigarette. I wondered what he saw.

For R.T. Bullock, the nightmares were easier to handle when he was out here. Down range so to speak. Only when he was in San Diego did life or death start to catch up to him. This was where he had chosen to feel comfortable. And he did on most days, especially work days.

But days like today were wait days. Hell, he had seen days like today turn out as a full firefight in seconds. One mortar, one sniper, or car bomb, and it's lose-your-buddy time. Simply a fact of life, he thought.

The cigarette he smoked was the first one in six months, and it would be the last. He had decided to quit. She hated him to smoke anyway. But quitting to please her was just not how he did things. Anna, oh Anna, could she ever be able to handle him, quit this or quit that and we can be happy?

"Hell, I'm happy now!" R.T. thought. "Maybe quit Anna and stay happy. No silly nightclubs and hanging out with her uptight friends. I'd lot rather be here right here. After all, people back home don't have a clue about reality. They live in a fairytale! Plenty of food, clothes, and a solidly false sense of security. They know nothing about the rest of the world.

The hardest thing for Anna in a day is deciding what to wear to the club at night. Hell, I'm done with her! I can get love out of my job, and sex is highly overrated anyway." R.T. drew one last pull from his cigarette and tossed it out onto the sand.

From my tent I could see the man toss his cigarette into the dirt. I wondered if the man was a SEAL, because most SEALs didn't smoke. For us pilots only the old men smoke. As for me, I couldn't stand the thoughts of inhaling million of filthy particles into my lungs. With that thought I took out a wet wipe and cleaned my hands and face.

Before I could finish pulling the moist towel across my face, I felt the concussion. Then the BOOOOMMMMM!!!!

The explosion shook the ground, I fell on my face, dazed. I looked around to see how close the blast was. I ran the totals: Gun in holster under arm, good; gas mask, in hand and about to be on, good; ears ringing, bad; tingling in arms, bad; no sign of blood on me, good! Sum of totals, good.

As I sealed my gas mask and stood up, I noticed a group forming at the end of the camp. I knew what it was before I even looked. A stretcher team was putting parts of desert camo fatigues on a stretcher. I could see what I thought were three bodies, one completely in half, one missing a leg.

I would find out later that an experienced lieutenant and two others were trying to disarm a land mind and lost. I looked back over at the SEAL tent. The man was still sitting in his chair leaning back against the tent.

CHAPTER TEN
Reality

Alexandria could see the explosion as she flew her daily mail delivery to our camp.

After landing and stowing her helmet and gear, she walked past the area where moments before three men were ripped apart by the explosion of the mine. Only glancing over at the stretchers, she asked, "Are you in one piece?"

"I am, but others aren't that lucky. Land mines are unforgiving. Here it's a constant barrage of boredom followed by terror," I said, dismayed at what I had witnessed.

"That is a fact! Could you imagine not knowing anything else but this?" she said.

I had never looked at it that way. I always knew that I was just visiting and would be going home sooner or later, never imagining how locals must think and feel.

"That is a bleak thought" I said.

"In Holland we have it so good, it is hard for any Dutch to think this sort of thing is really happening. Sure the T.V shows it, but it doesn't have the feel of reality."

"I understand. Americans are also disconnected from the absoluteness of this life.

"I guess that's why they say war is hell!" I said looking back at her.

"It's the children that have to decide to change it," she said as she stared into the distance.

I was again taken back by her beauty. Her black hair and dark skin were not the typical features of the Dutch. But she was not just lovely to look at, she had a warmness that radiated from within. She cared.

I tried to keep telling myself that even camels were attractive after four months in the desert and not to get carried away. But camels didn't have the soft curves just beneath a flight suit that said she was all the woman any man could handle in one lifetime.

"Do you have children?" she asked.

"Yes," I said.

"Would you ever have more?" she asked.

"Maybe, with the right person. I'm sort of down on relationships right now," I said and explained about my wife sending me separation papers.

She removed her stare from far away and settled her eyes on mine.

"How do you feel about that?" she asked softly.

That was a hard question to answer. I had spent so many days in anguish over my wife. Arguing about everything, being hurt time after time. There was always some issue unresolved and irresolvable. But I never had thought it would be the way it was. But the reality of it was almost a relief. I would not take her back now. I would no longer feel hurt, as I have been handed a final decision from my heart.

"I feel numb," I said, looking off across the desert.

"Will you go back to her?" she asked.

"I will go to see my children, but as for her, something in me has changed here. I am not the boy I was that kept taking it on the chin. All the petty arguments can be argued with herself. She can flirt and date without my being troubled. I have decided to give her what she really wants, a life that does not include me or the U.S. Army." I said.

Alex looked at me and then down at her hands. She picked at her nails.

"Lance, I don't usually say this sort of thing or show my feelings. I wouldn't now if I had more time to play it out. But time and events as they are, I will say this. I haven't even as much as looked at a man in years. I was

91

hurt once and wrote men off. Then you came along, and although we've just known each other a couple of days, I feel like I've known you all my life.

"Lance, I go back to Holland tomorrow. And if by some chance you ever think about me after I'm gone, I would like to see you again." She said as she looked up. "Tomorrow?" I said, stunned.

"Yes, I just found out and came to say goodbye," her bottom lip was trembling.

"Your kidding me!" I said, but knew there was no kidding in a trembling lip.

"I wish I were. Lance, you have been a good friend. I will never forget you. Please come to Holland and visit," she said, trying to push back a tear.

"Write me," I said.

"Everyday I will write you so you will know someone wants you to make it home." She gave me a peck on the lip, turned and walked away.

I watched her helicopter until it disappeared in the blue sky.

As promised, a couple of weeks later I received a letter from Alex. And she continued to write me everyday until I went home.

CHAPTER ELEVEN
Mere Mortals

The flies circled my plate as my right arm subconsciously fanned them away like the tail of a cow discouraging flies from her back.

The flies seemed to materialize out of thin air. Each one buzzed as it made a low pass by my face then down across my plate. The single buzz became a unified swarming sound. I was sure these were the same flies that frequented the poop tent, medical waste area, and the bodies left to rot around the local area. Now they are here on final approach to my plate.

The days were long as we continued to gather to contemplate some of life's greatest questions and our own destinies.

As far as religion, I had always had a basic belief in God even though many questions haunted me about the Bible. Hard questions. Questions like: if God is, how can he let little children suffer at the hands of evil? And why is it that those that do good always get punished? Case in point, Jesus. Although these questions lingered in the back of my mind, I still believed. It was not until the war that I could see the entire picture. The picture became very clear as I edged closer to my mortality. As pilots we felt invincible. Sure our friends crashed and got shot down and killed, but we believed it was because they were in error in their piloting skills, or made a mistake, pilot error. We simply believed we were better and that is why we were alive and they weren't. The army looked for self-confidence as a prerequisite. Self-confidence beyond basic-self confidence. something down the line of shear crazy with an immortal faith in self.

Rob Wind was a born-again Christian with a mission to change us all. We were believers to a point--the point being as long as we could curse, chase wild women, kill whoever got in our way, fight and drink. I did it all, except the drinking. I never liked the drinking part. Being out of control was not my idea of a good time. And I only chased those wild women while I was single.

My grandfather, with whom I spent much of my youth, instilled in me some basic values. Don't drink, don't mess around on your wife, and trust Jesus. Everyday he would read the Bible. At the time it sounded foreign and not applicable to my life, but the more I lived, the closer to home the words were. He gave me a valuable foundation on which to build my life.

We called Rob the preacher. He would silently protest our language by walking out of the tent when the cursing began. Rob lived like a saint but flew like the devil. Among all of us, Rob was the craziest and took more chances. Calm and easy going in day-to-day activities, he was a true terror in the cockpit. He would fly lower, faster, closer to the mountains than anyone else. His eyes had a certain easiness that looked on you with caring and true friendship. We always knew Rob cared. He would do anything for us, just ask. But he constantly questioned us, "Do you know Jesus? Are you saved?" So the rest of the guys steered clear of Rob.

The old men always gave Rob a hard time.

"How in the hell can you fly attack helicopters and preach?"

"God had warriors!" Rob would answer.

"Do you feel you are sinning by the killing the enemy?" Rob asked the question.

"Hell, killing is killing," John answered as he lit a cigarette and took a long puff.

"So you are telling me there is no difference between killing in war and killing someone for the fun of it?" Ron asked.

"If it wasn't fun, I wouldn't be here." John said, looking up with a slight grin.

"Killing is never fun," Rob answered. "But we are ordered to do it."

John was incredulous.

"So you are telling me as long as we are ordered to do it, it is okay?"

"Sure, God has ordered countries to go to war, and if it is not God's will, then the politicians will carry the sin."

"Hell will be full of politicians then." John said.

"Especially from Vietnam."

Suddenly Bugs jumped in, "Damn John, you old farts always see the world through the Vietnam visor. Shit, this is a different war, different cause, different reason. We are different."

"That is a lie; we are no different. We are the same. Only the faces and names here changed. Wars simply come and go for different reasons, but we warriors have been the same since the beginning of time. It's the leaders that get corrupt, either in our country or theirs!" John took another draw on his cigarette and thumped it out onto the sand.

"The bottom line is, if we win we live, if we lose we die. So we fight to win," Bugs said.

"So I'm going to smoke as many of those ragheads as I can."

"Do you think they can get to our homeland?"

"Sooner or later, these radical camel jockeys will figure out that they can easily hit the homeland. And when they do, watch out, we will be like Israel hit by a suicide bomber every week. So I'm going to hit them here, now. If we had any sense we would go ahead and hit Iran, Syria, and all the rest of them while the cards are in our favor. If we hit them now, it will put them behind by twenty years and they will never catch up enough to be a factor." Bugs said as he leaned back in his chair.

"Yes, all our government is going to do is blow up some building and then spend millions to rebuild, all the time never gaining the respect of these people," John says putting out another cigarette.

"People don't respect big shots bringing in foreign workers to rebuild their countries. They respect Apaches kicking their butts!" Bugs said.

"You all worry about the wrong things. Worry about your souls. Because if you die tonight, your role is over, none of this will matter. The only thing that will matter is what happens to your soul. So be ready now," Rob said.

Everyone turned and looked at Rob.

"It's true guys, at any time anyone one of us can be called. The question is, are you ready?"

" So preacher, tell me if there is a God and he is good and great, then why do we have wars and the children suffer?" Bugs asked.

I looked over at Bugs and wondered if he was a mind-reader. This was the question I have wanted to ask for years.

"See guys, its not about us, it's not about any of this. All of this has already been written, we know how it will end. It's about God and his will, and if we will find him among all this craziness and accept him." Rob continued.

"If you live your entire life with everything you want: cars, houses, food, love, no suffering, and end up going to hell; or if you suffer your entire life and accept God and go to heaven. Which is worse? Our life is just a breath; eternity is forever. So if a child in its short life, suffers, then goes to be with God in Heaven, then the child is forever in Glory." Rob reasoned.

"You see, this world is not important. It's sort of like a big game board to see who will accept the true God and his son Jesus. Our life in this world is simply designed to separate the wheat from the weeds. The weeds are thrown into the fire. So which are you? A weed or wheat? If you trust in him he will give you comfort." Rob stood up with his arms wide and his palms up as if he was a Baptist preacher calling for sinners.

Everyone was silent in thought.

There are many types of prayer, I thought. Those quick, "thank you for our food," increasing in intensity up to, "Oh God, please save me!"

For some reason I never felt really afraid in the middle of an attack when the bullets were flying. However, given a few days to think about it, I become terrorized. And I prayed harder and more sincerely than the dinner blessing.

With each mission two things happened. First, I felt somewhat invincible by defeating the enemy and accomplishing a mission. Secondly, fear crept into my mind with each image of a fellow American's body parts.

I kept telling myself that he made a mistake, pilot error; it was his time. Then that feeling of my own mortality ran under the door of my mind like a thick liquid. And with that fear, ever so slight, came the need to induce a heavier more sincere prayer. Just in case I ended up in more than one piece, I wanted my maker to reassemble me.

CHAPTER TWELVE
Hunter

For R.T. there was no real relationship or love, nothing but the Navy and the teams. As for letters from home, they had stopped years ago.

The folks back home talked of him as a sailor that was "over there doing something". R.T. never really thought of them. The last time he was home had been ten years ago at a high school reunion.

He listened to some old school mates, now rednecks, talk of how tough they were, and their adventures in the deer woods, as if they could somehow measure their manhood by the points on a deer's antlers. One of them turned to R.T. and asked, "Do you still hunt or has the navy made you a soft city boy?"

He decided then and there never to go back. Not because he really disliked his old schoolmates, but because their level of life experiences were not worth the time.

And besides, they would not understand. Somewhere in the back of his mind he hoped they would never know what a real hunt was about. A hunt where the hunter could just as easily be the hunted. Where there was killing. Not just sport but survival. A situation some politician dream up but turned out to be a disaster leaving you running for your life shooting everything, killing everything. Surviving.

R.T. held the black frame of the Beretta pistol in his hand. Touching it quick and light, cleaning it, checking it, and cleaning it again, this was his friend, his lifeline. He quickly put it back together, his hands moving as they had thousands of times: parts, metal sounds, moving together, back to form a working, clean pistol. The bullets were each examined, placed in the magazine until it was full, packed another magazine, slapped it into the Beretta, slid it away in his holster awaiting the next quick touch of his hand.

R.T. had a certain ritual before every mission: it started with his weapons and ended with a prayer. R.T.'s prayers were different from most of the normal church people back in his home town. For at his church they had the luxury every Sunday of sitting in a comfortable building, listening to a sermon, with no real danger at hand. They could make a decision to wait until next Sunday to accept the salvation of Jesus. For R.T., this was it, alter time, accept or reject salvation now. Later may never come.

With the sun sinking into the horizon, the darkness covered our camp like a blanket. Outside the gates in the daylight there were only shepherds and sheep. After darkness fell, the sheep turned into terrorists and began shooting.

RAP! RAP! RAP! BZZZ! BZZZ! Rounds could be heard impacting the concrete building. Matt hit the start switch to engine number one and the whine of the first engine sounded in my helmet earphone. As engine one reached idle speed, Matt fingered the number-two start switch. Both engines matched.

A young marine's voice crackled over the QRF frequency, "We are rolling, taking fire from the north!"

In the distance I could see streams of tracer rounds hitting our camps embankment.

"I'm ready. Power leverage to fly," Matt said.

I flipped my helmet display unit over my right eye.

"On go, good before take off check, and we are off," I said.

I pulled the Apache into the air, I pressed the left pedal, rotating the nose to orient on the area where the tracers were originating. My right thumb selected the 30mm cannon as my right index finger pressed the trigger to the first detent, activating the laser range finder. Focusing my right eye on some white heat signatures where the tracers were originating, I selected zoom, and instantly identified men with AK 47 rifles. My index finger pressed the trigger to the second detent sending a ten-round burst of 30mm slamming into the soft bodies of the terrorists.

"Good hit! Good hit!" came the marine's voice in my earphones.

"I guess for somebody, we provided comfort," Matt said.

At the same time Matt and I were providing comfort to the marines on the perimeter, R.T. was stepping out of a Blackhawk helicopter. He and two other SEALS were on the move to set in motion a mission that Matt and I were to finish two days later...

The SEALs moved in the night to a remote location overlooking a fort used by the Iraqi military. The fort had several pieces of equipment used by the Iraqis to terrorize the Kurdish. Protecting the fort were several antiaircraft 30mm guns, positioned to give our helicopters a bad day.

After three days of hiking in the mountains, the SEALS were in place and ready. R,T, opened a case holding a long tube-looking gun. This gun was very unique because it didn't shoot bullets; it shot a laser. This special laser was on the same frequency as the hellfire missile hanging on the rail of my Apache.

It was now night and Matt and I were hovering five miles away from R.T. and the fort. The Apache's rotors cause a constant vibration in my seat as it floated over the rough rocks behind the crest of the hill in front of me. Matt and I were completely hidden here and awaiting a call from the SEALs' team.

As I checked my position on the map, my earphone crackled to life, "Dragonfly this is skull, lights are on."

This told me that R.T. had spotted a target and the laser was marking it. I pressed a button, slaving one of my hellfire laser-guided missiles to the marked target.

"One missile Alpha code, left rail, ready for launch. On your command," I said over the satellite-secure radio.

"Fire, spot on!" R.T. replied.

I squeezed the trigger. A bright flash lit up the left side of the aircraft as the missile left the rail and arched upward over the hill in front of the my aircraft. Five miles away, a small spot appeared in the sky. The spot got brighter, looking like a falling star as the hellfire glided towards the fort. A bright flash was followed by a loud rumble that resonated and echoed off the nearby mountains. One of the tanks in the fort compound was now no more than a heap of scrap metal.

"Good hit! Send me two, fire spot on!" R.T. was watching the show as we sat five miles away. Now he was asking for two missiles at one time. I selected two more missiles and called R.T.

"Two alpha code, ten second delay. One shot out now!" I said pressing the trigger.

Once again a bright flash, and the missiles disappear over the hill. I waited ten seconds and pressed the trigger again. The next hellfire left the rail. Now two missiles were inbound to the fort. R.T. pointed the laser at another tank. The hellfire slammed into the armor, spewing fire and metal into the air with a bright flash.

R.T. moved the laser to another vehicle as the second hellfire rode the laser beam into the vehicle. The flash sent shadows to the mountains surrounding the fort.

"Good hit! Thanks for the package. Skull out!" R.T. said over the secure line as he began packing up to move out.

Matt and I swung the nose of the Apache to head home.

"Another night at the office!" Matt said.

"I don't know about you, but I'm hungry, I said as my stomach grumbled.

R.T. had a day walk to his pickup point.

Matt and I flew back to the base, had a MRE, and played a game of chess.

CHAPTER THIRTEEN
Goodbye to Hell

The sandy wind blew in the tent flap behind the captain. The news was new and shocking, almost sending a numb feeling through my body. I thought it was a joke.

"Luke, you and Matt are out of here in the morning!" he said.

"Sir?" I said, not understanding.

"You're out of here in the morning! You're going home. Our mission here is over. We are sending two pilots home everyday. And you and Matt are next!" he said with a smile.

I looked over at Matt. He was already packing.

"When am I going?" Bugs asked.

"Oh, you are going home with them!" The captain said.

"It's about time!" Bugs said.

"The old men left this morning. Everybody will be home within a couple of weeks."

I followed Matt's lead and began packing. I didn't sleep all night.

The next morning we boarded a large CH47 Chinook helicopter which would fly us to Insurlik Airbase in Turkey. At the moment I was so happy to be going home I didn't realize that I actually was leaving Iraq for good.

At Insurlik we caught a C-130 to Germany.

Just like that we were back home.

When I arrived in Germany, the house was empty. My wife had decided to go back to the United States months before officially leaving me. All the furniture was gone; all the money in the bank was gone. I was cleaned out. In the center of the empty living room was a single toy left on the floor with a note. It read,

"You will miss us."

She had taken my two boys ages six and three. Gone. Empty was my house and my heart. Not so much for her anymore, but for my children. I wouldn't see them again for two years.

Two Weeks Later

As loneliness set it, I decided to go to Holland. When she opened the door, I smiled.

"So you did make it! I figured you had forgot about me!" Alexandria said.

"Thank you for writing me; it helped a great deal," I said.

"You know that the Dutch always do what they say," she said.

I hugged here for at least five minutes. She knew how it felt to return from a war.

We spent the next two days sightseeing in Holland. We talked for hours about life and the war. She was and is a good friend to this day. As far as a romantic relationship, maybe I wasn't ready or maybe she wasn't ready, but we decided that friends are much closer and more reliable than lovers. I have stayed in close contact with Alexandria until this day. As always, time slowly pushed us apart and our path led off in opposite directions.

Two years passed slowly in Germany. Flight missions were boring compared to the war. The practice and training were simply not combat. Spend a month at the range shooting. Spend another month in France on some gunnery exercise. Every month there was some mission to play war. We would pack up all our things and go camp in the woods playing Army. It was always wet and cold. The Army life became a drudge. The flying was nothing compared to the war experience. I was so depressed from my pain and the daily Army life. My medical problems were beginning to affect me. Not knowing what was wrong with me I withdrew. I actually hated to go fly. All our flights were at night. Some days I would feel so tired as if I was drugged. The chronic fatigue was settling into my body. The cold wet weather made the days dreary. My only bright spot was a young German girl named Nicole. Everyday after work I would head to her house. She was there for me for my last two years in Germany. I called her my Elf Princess. Her family sort of adopted me. They were the best experience I had in Europe. We traveled and spent hours simply talking.

When I left Germany, I fully intended to marry her and bring her home with me. As life would have it, the situation in America did not become the great welcome home I expected. I thought for sure after all of my training and experience, I would easily acquire a high-paying job and be able to support Nicole. It wasn't to be. When I arrived back in the States, all I could think of was Nicole's family. She was her dads little girl. It would crush him for her to move to the States. I just couldn't breakup that wonderful family. So I would put off bringing her over. Days turned to weeks, weeks turned to months. Now it has been years. I have thought of her many times since I left Germany. Now we both have a different life. I have now married and have two beautiful little girls with my wife. Sometimes when I look at my daughters I think of the love between Nicole and her dad. They are special people. I will never forget them.

CHAPTER FOURTEEN
Welcome Home

Europe was beautiful from ten thousand feet as our 747 bounced among the clouds. My ticket was marked Nuremberg to Jacksonville.

My window seat gave me a view that was priceless. The countryside was stretched out below like the tapestry of one of grandmother's quilts. With the looks and charm of a medieval story land, the castles of long ago still stood proud on the hilltops overlooking the local villages. My mind's eye could almost see the knights riding down from the fortress out into the hilly countryside to rescue the villagers from the evil dragons. I sadly thought of all the dragons I had met since I left home. I guess the real dragons are never killed by the knights, they just change forms through the centuries.

How did I ever get involved in such things as flying and wars? Dad didn't want me to join; mom didn't want me to join. Maybe it was that farm and the thought of never going anywhere or doing anything. I was more afraid of being a nobody than of dying. I wanted to stand for something more than I was. Be something more. I couldn't see myself driving a truck or working in a store for thirty years. Or being fat at forty and dying from a heart attack before I was sixty with little to show for my life.

It had been important to me to serve my country, right some wrongs, stand for the weak, do my part for the good fight. When I was a boy on the farm, it was just work, work, work. But I was safe and comfortable. When I was old enough to realize that others were in harm's way protecting my comfort, I had to go. Now I longed for that farm.

For many reasons my mind was happy, but my heart was heavy with an aching sadness. I left many wonderful friends behind in Germany and in the army. No matter how hard things seemed to be at the time, I had met many good people and learned more than any one school or college could have ever taught me.

The haunting question of what I would do next burdened my mind for most of the flight home. I could never give up flying the Apache, so I would join the Florida Guard when I got home. Maybe even fly for a sheriff's department. My heart also ached for my Elf Princess

(Nicole). I missed her. She was my best friend for the last two years. I kept telling myself, After I get everything ready I will bring her over. After arriving home I quickly realized that America was cruel. Especially to a foreigner. A young girl with a German accent would be made fun of and treated poorly. I was an Apache pilot with combat medals, which I thought was a big deal. Still some in my home town asked "Why did the Army kick you out?" I certainly didn't get kicked out, but I did feel like I was kicked in the teeth from some of my hometown folks after arriving home. Many hometown people welcomed me home but others were somewhat hateful. "Why did you get out of the Army?" "Are you crazy"? "Are you shell shocked?" "Did you get to kill a bunch of Iraqis?" "When are you going to settle down and keep a job?" People were sometimes hateful. There was no way I would ever bring my Elf Princess back here.

Job Interview, 1993, Florida

"Mr. Neeley will see you now!" I was lost in my thoughts.

"Mr. Walker, Mr. Walker, you're next!" The secretary's soft voice encroached upon my daydream as her pretty face comes into focus.

"Mr. Walker? You're next!"

113

After several hour's wait in a line of twenty-nine other police officer want-to-be's, it's my turn.

I adjusted my suit and entered the interview room. Sitting behind his desk, arms folded, leaning back in his chair, the overweight officer in charge of new recruits by-passed all the formalities of a normal interview and cut directly to the chase.

"Mr. Walker we are looking for police officers." I nodded.

"We do have several helicopters, but we get all our pilots from the force," he shuffled through some papers on his desk.

"What did you fly anyway?" he asked as he squinted to read my 201 military file.

"Apaches." I replied.

"What is that?"

From that simple question, I knew this job would be a long shot.

"It's the army's most advanced attack helicopter," I explained, wanting to add things like, "It can kill an enemy tank five miles away in bad weather at night."

"Whatever an Apache is, we don't have any here, and if we did, we would want you to be in a black and white for at least three years before you start flying,"

I leaned back in the chair and wondered one more time, why was I here?

"Sir, how many hours of flying time do your pilots have?" I asked, trying to gain some ground on my experience. Having been a Warrant Officer, I was always taught to be prepared.

I had researched this police department. I knew that they had two pilots and three helicopters. One pilot had 1,500 flight hours and the other had all of 300 hours. Neither pilot had any prior time in the Bell 206, which was the helicopter used by this force.

"I'm sure they've both had hundreds of hours. They both are good police officers."

He looked up from the papers directly into my eyes with a stern look.

"Why do military guys always think they are better trained than our police force trainees?" he snapped.

I stared back at him for a second, then smiled.

"Sir, I didn't mean to imply that your pilots aren't trained well. I have never flown with either of them. I wish I could, because I need a job."

He leaned forward and unfolded his arms. "Mr. Walker, I will keep you in mind, but please realize we also send about thirty students to the police academy every six months for a future job with us."

I thanked him for his time.

As I drove home, I thought again of Matt, Bugs, and the old men and wonder if maybe they were right. Maybe

I should have stayed in and retired. Maybe there was no place in civilian life for an attack pilot. Had I made a mistake? Who in their right mind would give up the best job in the world? I thought I was losing it. Going crazy maybe. No. Just tired. Really tired.

The next morning, the clock radio woke me with the news of American peacekeepers on their way to Bosnia. I turned the radio down, stumbled to the bathroom, rinsed my face and looked into the mirror.

Since my Gulf War experience, there hadn't been a day that went by that I didn't think of how good things were here at home. I had a flushable toilet, running hot water, and just about anything else I needed. It had been just me for so long that female company wasn't so much a need anymore as it was a luxury.

The mirror reflected the image of a thirty-one-year-old man with boyish looks. But the years and the miles, not yet shown in my face, had permanently aged my mind. As for my hair, well, that was the only visible scar from the war. Maybe the stress, or simply the mileage. If I could have deleted all the images, I would. But they kept coming back. Sometimes they would sneak in to say hello in my dreams, or they would show up in the middle of the day to slap me in the face, leaving me with tears streaming. "I'm sure I'm one of the lucky ones; I made it home alive."

As clouds formed outside for a morning shower, they also began to form in my mind. There was again that faint smell of trash burning somewhere. I closed my eyes to wash my face. There she was, slumped over holding her baby. I opened my eyes as the warm water splashed across my face from my cupped hands. The burnt smell still lingered, and the body charred in the vehicle flashed across my mind. I splashed another hand full of water across my face, closing my eyes, ready for the horror, but there was nothing. Gone, but they would certainly return later.

I spent the rest of the morning wondering what I would do about a job and how I would pay the bills and child support. I was sure anyone would want a previous warrant officer and Apache pilot as an employee. I was wrong. Had I wasted my youth? Should I have joined the Army and followed the crazy dream of flying only to get out and lose all I have earned there. My mind fluttered like a flag in a strong wind. A chill came over my body, then a sweat.

The Iraqi children stood in the streets and begged, "Food mister, food!"

God I'm losing it. I've got to clear all this in my mind. I fought back the images of bodies and starving children. I told myself, no regrets. God put me here and made me like I am, so no regrets.

I picked up a pen and sat there, thinking. The pen began across the paper:

No regrets
And in my old age
I will look back on my life
And be glad it's the way it is.
For I am a mere mortal
With the foresight of such,
But if I did not do my heart's call,
I know in my old age I will pray to be given
Just one more chance to turn back the clock
To the days of my youth.
And in my days of youth I will have
The strength, courage, and wonder enough
To take the chance to be happy in my heart,
Satisfied in my mind,
And together with my true love.....

CHAPTER FIFTEEN
What's Left

After spending ten years in civilian life struggling to fit in and find a job, I finally settled into selling cars and mobile homes in North Florida. I even worked as a deputy sheriff in my home county for a short time. I had medical problems since I returned from the Gulf war, but didn't want to mention them. I would actually try to hide or suppress them. Admitting to any medical problems means no more flying career. I knew my concentration was not good enough to be a Apache pilot anymore. I could feel myself slipping. My muscles were constantly cramping. I would be so tired from average days of exercise. I would have flashbacks on a daily basis, leaving me with feelings of anxiety and paranoia. So I left the Army. No job ever could match being an Apache pilot. The selling jobs were a sort of reckless financial risk of success and failure, giving me a challenge. They paid the bills but always left me running out to see any helicopter flying low overhead. I decided to go back to flying, but when I did, my medical problems grounded me. My arms would become numb, my mind would drift, and I would lose concentration on critical task.

Not knowing what was wrong with me and fearing I would lose my medical certificate, I kept my problems a secret. My secret became worse.

Like a sly mountain lion, it slowly stalked me, then it attacked. When it finally started to disable me, it hit me hard. Late one summer afternoon, I was cleaning up the yard, burning some trash and the remnants of a dead animal my dog had dragged into the yard the previous night. The fire was consuming plastic and dead animal, sending a black smoke across the yard. The hot summer breeze blew in over an open field sending sand into my face and eyes. I rubbed my eyes. The trees faded to bright brown hills. The air around me felt like an oven. My tennis shoes were now desert boots, and a dusty scarf was around my neck. My flight suit replaced my blue jeans and tee shirt. The smell of flesh burning mixed with the burnt plastic smell of a vehicle. I was transposed from my back yard to Iraq in seconds. I rubbed my eyes, thinking it would go away. When I opened my eyes again, obscure in my view but the image showing through the smoke is no where in site.

Sweat formed across my face and around my body where my flight suit sleeves were rolled up. Flies were buzzing everywhere, most would try to get into my face. I swatted at the flies and squinted at the smoke. I began to choke from the smoke and dust. My mouth was as dry as a cotton ball. A drop of water to my mouth, just a drop. When I reached to check my Beretta, my hand landed in the spot where my Beretta was supposed to be. Empty, nothing, no steel. Sweat ran down my sideburns, making a stream across my dry cheeks. My left hand continues its search for the cold steel of my weapon, but still no Beretta! Where is it? Did I lose it? My left hand patted under my right shoulder, feeling for the familiar handle. Nothing! Nothing! My hand moved to my rib cage, feeling my tee-shirt. There was no weapon. There were no flies. The brown hills in the distance were now green trees. What was going on? Where was I? I fell down on the ground and looked around, trying to piece together my memory and my present position in time. As quickly as it had come, it was gone, leaving me exhausted and shaken.

Present Day

As time passes, the frequency of the events increase. Sneaking in sometimes to paralyze my senses, other times just a slight hello from the past to leave me shaking in the corner of my bedroom at 3 a.m. It never stops. It is like a living a nightmare.

I never realized it at the time, but Matt and I were also physically injured, maybe even fatally. It seems our bodies were invaded by something that was degrading our nervous, muscular, and mental systems. Some call it Gulf War Syndrome: others say it is caused by radiation from the weapons we used or nerve agent we came in contact with. At first, I thought it was a bunch of bull and that I was simply tired. But as my pain increased, I knew something was trashing my body. I have always been a world-class athlete, able to run two mile in 11 minutes. Now, the pain shows up and bends me double with muscle spasms and cramps.

I sleep for days at a time to recover from simple everyday activities. Attacked from within, my body counters each salvo of pain with fatigue. My guts ache. My muscles ache. My head aches to the point of dizziness. My mind slips into other times and places, carrying my conscious like a helpless passenger along for the ride. Sometimes I forget what year it is or where I am. I have been lost in my back yard.

Many who knew me before realize that something is wrong and whisper as I pass. Once sharp and precise, now my mind is darken with indecision. I stare at blank pages with no words left to apply to those pages. Headaches blister my mind leaving large boils of hallucinating thoughts. Fatigue clings to my body and mind like a large anchor it which I must drag. At one time in my youth I thought pain was a mere thought only weak minded people dwelled on. Now I know it as a hungry gator tearing my muscles with cramps and spasms. Who knows how long it will last today, or when it will leave tomorrow. I just brace for what is to come. And I feel as if I am circling the fields of Autumn tiring with each flap of my weary wings. And through it all I pray. The prayer like one prays in pain. Like one prays when it counts. When the enemy is closing in and the ammo is short. The gun is laid down and the knife is slid from its scabbard. The last line of defense. When nothing can help but the mighty hand of God. God, Please, HELP ME!

And like always his gentle hand is there. I am blessed with a beautiful wife sent from the Almighty. She serves her country by taking care of her vet, and it is a difficult job. She struggles with my moods and drifts of mind and body. She is a true soldier, rescuing me from my battle daily. She has helped me finish this book. She collected my old notes and writings to compile these words. Her patience and understanding is beyond that of a mortal. Thank you Lord for her.

Even though I am disabled, I am thankful. For many will never know the feeling of hovering an Apache or the thrill of flying at night in combat. Many will never really live their dreams. Some exist and never live; I have lived and now exist. I have paid a heavy price.

When I left Iraq and the military, I thought my fight was over. No, it has simply moved within. Some days the fight is in my mind; other days, in my muscles.

My wife, Kim, and my five children are always at my side even during my bad days. God has been there for me through it all, and when I was at my lowest, he sent me a wonderful wife and five great children. Once again He is providing comfort.

CHAPTER SIXTEEN
The Challenge

He was not of this life, maybe an angel or an advanced soul. I could tell it by the look in his eyes; they were bright with a fire that burned from the soul.

As he approached with quick steps, he scanned the entire scene and looked directly into my eyes as if to read my mind and soul.

He knew my heart and thus he spoke like an old friend. I felt I had known him for a lifetime.

"Why are you a speaker and do not speak?"

I wasn't sure what to say.

He pressed on, "Why are you a romantic without a love?"

My mouth was sealed, knowing I should only listen to his questions.

"Are you are a fighter without a fight?" His eyes were so bright that my eyes watered, but I could not look away.

The questions continued,

"Are you a hunter that will not kill? A knight with no dragon?

"Is your sword not as sharp as any ever?" he asked forcefully as his eyes blazed an inscription on my heart.

Even though he possessed all power, I was not afraid, for I knew he was here to help me.

So I spoke the only words I could find.

"Why me?" I asked.

His eyes seemed to cool for a brief second and he touched my shoulder.

His hand had so much energy I felt faint from the warmth.

His voice mellowed,

"You were born a warrior; your sword, my friend, is of your choosing. Your fight is within. Stand on the rock of your soul, the rock of morals. Use your sharpest dagger, your wisdom! Draw passion from your heart, fueled by the fire of your spirit. Fight for your beliefs. Everything around you could give way or fail, but not your true beliefs."

My pillow was wet when I awoke. The question I had asked so many times before,

"What am I to do," now I had an answer.

The pen is truly mightier than the sword. For with the pen lives have been taken and lives have been spared. With the pen, we can reach special friends. The pen can give us a gift worth keeping.

May you find a gift...

ABOUT THE AUTHOR

Lance Walker now survives in his home town of Branford Florida with his wife and children. He has never flown again.

SPECIAL THANKS

There are always special people that live in our thoughts to guide us along our journey. Those that shared some of their special knowledge and wisdom to make us better people. Many have helped and trained me. My family Mom, Dad, Step parents, and Grandparents were all special. There were also others. In which I can never forget.

Special Thanks to all my teachers that taught me the best way to fly is use my wings. Rudy Glover, Ross Sears, Mary Daniels, Willie Veal, Katherine Melnick, Mrs. Humphreys, Coach Alford, Bob Barnes and all the other teachers and instructors on my journey.

Also a very special thanks to the Kraus family for taking care of me in Germany. You are always in my thoughts.

It seems at every point along my journey, these special people were there at that perfect time to give me inspiration.

Providing Comfort…Thank you!

Printed in the United States
71900LV00001B/31-138

9 781425 972103